CHAKRA HEALING

Inspiring | Educating | Creating | Entertaining

Brimming with creative inspiration, how-to projects, and useful
information to enrich your everyday life, Quarto Knows is a favorite
destination for those pursuing their interests and passions. Visit our
site and dig deeper with our books into your area of interest:
Quarto Creates, Quarto Cooks, Quarto Homes, Quarto Lives,
Quarto Drives, Quarto Explores, Quarto Gifts, or Quarto Kids.

First published in 2019 by Wellfleet Press,
an imprint of The Quarto Group
142 West 36th Street, 4th Floor
New York, NY 10018 USA
T (212) 779-4972 **F** (212) 779-6058
www.QuartoKnows.com

10 9 8 7 6 5 4 3 2 1

ISBN: 978-1-57715-202-6

Cover and Interior Design: Ashley Prine, Tandem Books

Printed in China

This book provides general information on various widely known and widely accepted images that tend
to evoke feelings of strength and confidence. However, it should not be relied upon as recommending or
promoting any specific diagnosis or method of treatment for a particular condition, and it is not intended
as a substitute for medical advice or for direct diagnosis and treatment of a medical condition by a
qualified physician. Readers who have questions about a particular condition, possible treatments for that
condition, or possible reactions from the condition or its treatment should consult a physician or other
qualified healthcare professional.

IN FOCUS

CHAKRA HEALING

Your Personal Guide

ROBERTA VERNON

WELLFLEET
PRESS

CONTENTS

INTRODUCTION 6

PART I: THE CHAKRAS

CHAPTER ONE
All About Chakras . . . 12

CHAPTER TWO
The Major Chakras . . . 24

CHAPTER THREE
The Minor Chakras . . . 60

CHAPTER FOUR
Identifying Weak Chakras . . . 66

PART II: CHAKRA HEALING

CHAPTER FIVE
Working with Chakras: Energy and Spiritual Healing Basics . . . 82

CHAPTER SIX
Reiki Healing for Chakras . . . 90

CHAPTER SEVEN

Crystal Healing for Chakras . . . 96

CHAPTER EIGHT

Healing Chakras with Color . . . 104

CHAPTER NINE

Essential Oils for Chakras . . . 112

CHAPTER TEN

Healing Emotional
Pain Through Chakras . . . 116

CHAPTER ELEVEN

Magical and Meditative
Chakra Techniques . . . 122

CHAPTER TWELVE

Chakra Healing for Animals . . . 132

APPENDIX: CHAKRA CONNECTIONS 136

CONCLUSION 138

ABOUT THE AUTHOR 139

IMAGE CREDITS 140

INDEX 141

INTRODUCTION

This book is divided into two parts. The first teaches about the chakras—what they are and how to tell if there are any issues with them. The second explores different methods for healing chakras.

Chakra healing isn't a specific therapy. Rather, it is brought about by using techniques that work on the chakras. Each chakra refers to certain health, emotional, or spiritual conditions. The challenge is to find methods that bring about positive changes within the chakra system without doing any harm.

If you become ill or injured, you must go to an appropriate doctor, surgeon, hospital, or specialist and get conventional medical treatment. You also must use common sense. There are a number of complementary therapies that can help your body to recover and others that will help you to relax. Many of these methods can be directed toward the chakras, thus helping you to treat both physical ailments and emotional problems through the chakra system.

If you are receiving conventional medical treatment, remember to tell your doctor about any complementary therapies that you are also using, especially those that enter the body, such as homeopathy, herbal treatments, and aromatherapy. Complementary treatments such as reflexology and energy healing are less of a concern, but it still is worth mentioning them to your doctor.

Healing Methods in This Book

There are plenty of methods to choose from to heal chakras; crystal healing is an obvious one, as is Reiki. Chakras also respond well to color healing, say, by wrapping scarves around a client's shoulders while he asks his spirit guide for his problem to be taken away. Colored paper shapes, ribbons, crystals, and much else can be placed directly on the chakras, either by using the color associated with each chakra to give a boost of energy, or by using very pale blue or white to calm the chakras down. If the healer then brings white light down from the universe, it will encourage the healing colors to enter the chakras.

Massage with aromatherapy will help heal the chakras, and bringing essences into the atmosphere by burning them in a diffuser can also be useful. The challenge is in selecting an essence that is appropriate to the ailing chakra, such as a musky one to activate a sluggish base chakra, or a floral one to comfort a damaged heart chakra. It is even possible to put a flower essence on a particular chakra to cheer it up or to calm it down.

ALTERNATIVE THERAPIES

An *alternative* is something that "stands in place" of the usual methods. Where medical treatments are concerned, there always will be people who choose the alternative method in place of the conventional one. A good example is a person who goes to a specialist in Chinese medicine.

COMPLEMENTARY THERAPIES

Complementary means working "alongside" conventional medicine rather than replacing it, and nowadays there are many kinds of holistic therapists working in hospitals alongside conventional practitioners. Most of the concepts outlined in this book come into this category.

ENERGY HEALING

This type of healing can be very helpful. It works through the aura and the nervous system and through the chakras. Where serious illness is concerned, it isn't enough treatment on its own, but it speeds recovery, it is noninvasive, and it can be given at a distance.

A Note on Language

·····◆◆◆◆◆◆·····

In this book, I usually refer to the person who gives healing as the *healer*, but the person on the receiving end might be the *client* or *recipient* and, occasionally, the *patient*. I also call people *subjects*, *individuals*, and *persons* or *people* depending on the circumstances. If I have to talk about people in the singular, I use the words *he* and *him* to prevent the language from becoming awkward

Therapies that enter the chakras via the aura or the meridians (lines of energy that connect one part of the body to another) can help heal ailments, and these may come in the form of massage or treatments such as acupuncture, acupressure, emotional freedom technique, or my personal favorite—reflexology.

Using Buddhist, Christian, Jewish, Wiccan, Hindu, or any other form of chanting can be helpful, as can affirmations, mantras, or just plain sound, as long as it isn't discordant. Combining this with a restful meditation might be just the thing to open a slightly blocked chakra and help you think clearly.

So, by using this book for reference, you can look into health or emotional concerns that link with each chakra and you can choose to apply whatever healing method you favor.

✳ ✳ ✳

PART I
THE CHAKRAS

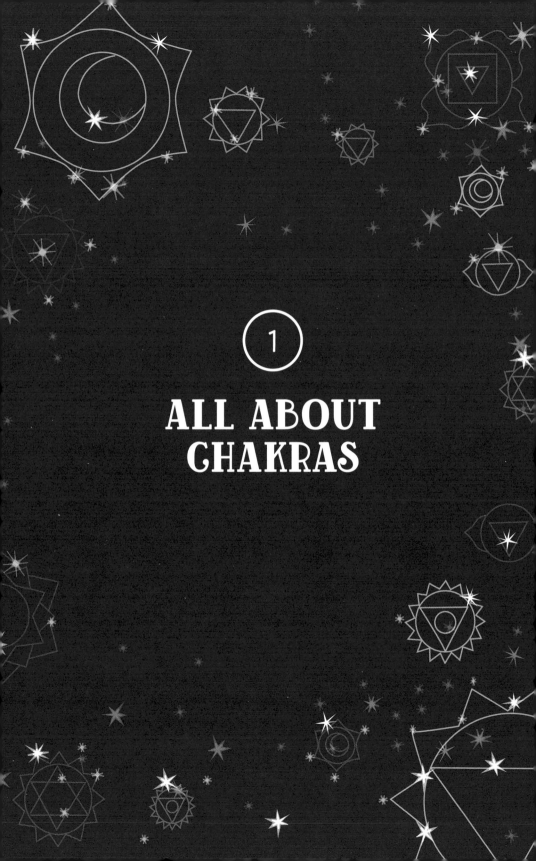

1

ALL ABOUT CHAKRAS

Chakra History

The word *chakra* comes from Sanskrit and means "wheel." The chakra system originated in India, and it is mentioned in four holy books that date back to before 2500 BCE, with other early references appearing in early writings called the *Upanishads*. Since then the system has become incorporated into Hinduism and Buddhism, later spreading to Tibet and, in recent years, to China and on to the West. In the Vedic (Hindu) tradition, the chakras are linked with the god Vishnu.

The Theosophical Society, formed in England in 1875, promotes universal brotherhood without distinction of race, creed, color, gender, or social background. It is based on the realization that life in all its diverse forms, human and nonhuman, is invisibly *One*. The Theosophists researched many Eastern ideas, including the chakras, working out their own concepts in relation to the chakras. Modern-day Indian students of the chakra system are in broad agreement with the Theosophists' ideas.

The arrival of the New Age, first in the USA in 1968 and later in the UK and Europe brought many of these old concepts to light. The ideas that proved to be workable and worth keeping have remained in use, and this includes the chakras.

Other traditions refer to connecting paths around the body, including the Chinese system of meridians (lines of energy that connect one part of the body to another) used in acupuncture, along with its spin-offs in the form of acupressure and reflexology. The aura is another subtle type of energy that surrounds the body in layers. There is even some similarity between the chakra system and the Kabala, and with ideas contained in Islamic Sufism.

What Is a Chakra?

A chakra is an energy center in the body that has energy flowing around it, but also through its center. There are seven main chakras in the body. The Hindu image of a chakra is that of two cones linked at the pointy or narrow ends, with the wide end of one cone opening in the front of the body and the other opening at the back. If the cone image is too awkward for you to envisage, imagine the chakras as tubes going through the body.

The chakras monitor the temperature and atmosphere around us, and they help us to know when we are too hot, too cold, too wet, or too dry. They link to the elements of fire, earth, air, and water, balancing our bodily functions to fit in with the world around us. They tell us when a place feels right for us or when it makes us feel uncomfortable, and whether the people we are with are likely to attack us or not. This isn't just in the sense of a watching out for muggers or thieves, but whether we feel comfortable with those with whom we work, our business contacts, and others with whom we have contact in our daily lives. Put simply, the chakras alert our sixth sense to tell us to fight or flee.

On a practical level, the chakras are linked to the condition of our bodies and the state of our minds, so if a chakra is partially or wholly blocked or misaligned, it is said to affect our health. Here one can take liberties with an ancient Latin saying that goes "*mens sana in corpore sano*," meaning "a healthy mind in a healthy body," and suggest that nice clear chakras help the mind and body to function properly.

The Three Levels

- At the basic level, the chakra system is linked to the physical body, thus dealing with such things as health, strength, sickness, weakness, and discomfort.

- The second level connects with the mind, the intellect, and the ego, along with the subtle concepts of intuition and sense. This level tells us that something is wrong, or alerts us to the fact that someone else is falling ill.

- The highest level relates to our spiritual nature, which allows us to contact the universe or the Almighty, but it can also help us to become psychic and mediumistic, and to get into contact with our spiritual guides. This level can even help us to tap into other people's past and future lives and to understand the nature and personality of others.

Chakras cannot be seen by an X-ray or an MRI scan, but they are part of the human body in the same way that the aura is. It is widely believed that chakras exist in the bodies of *all* living creatures. Those who have watched animals respond well to energy healing and to complementary therapies will find this easy to believe.

The chakras link with the endocrine system and the nerve ganglia that lie along the spinal column, and with the glands that supply us with the hormones that we need for life and for health. They monitor the world around us, checking for light, warmth, sound, smells, tastes, comfort, and discomfort, relating to the five traditionally recognized senses and the hidden senses of intuition and spirituality. The chakras sense changes in the weather and air pressure, and they let us know when our environment is set to become uncomfortable or even unsafe. They are part of our survival system.

That is why if a chakra is partially or wholly blocked, too open or misaligned, it can affect our state of mind and our health. At a more important level, a couple of badly functioning chakras could even affect our survival mechanism or our ability to spot danger before it arrives, so checking out the chakras and giving them healing can certainly be useful.

Chakras and the Aura

The aura is a layered field that surrounds humans and probably all animals as well. It is something like an electromagnetic field, but that is not it. Those who work with chakras may also work with the aura. Some say we shouldn't learn about the chakras or attempt to give them healing without knowing about, and working with, the aura, but the aura is a big subject of its own, so I won't go into it here, other than to touch on it where it is necessary for me to do so.

Chakras and Religion

Chakras are *not* a matter of belief, faith, or religion, and they do their job even if we refuse to believe chakras exist. However, if we want to give healing to others, it makes sense to believe in the existence of the chakras and to understand how they work.

How Many Chakras Are There?

Tradition tells us there are 78,000 chakras, but this is obviously an unworkable number, so we restrict ourselves to the seven main ones plus a number of minor ones that are worth considering from time to time. The extra chakras fall into three categories:

1. Two of the seven main chakras are said to be doubles, with one lying above the other.
2. There are several chakras that line up above the crown of the head.
3. There are a few other bodily chakras that seem to be important and active, such as those in the hands, shoulders, chest glands, hips, and feet.

The Seven Main Chakras

There is some discrepancy in the names of these chakras and also some confusion. For example, some people confuse the sacral and solar plexus chakra. It really doesn't matter what you call them, as they will still work by any name you call them.

1. The base chakra—also known as the root chakra
2. The sacral chakra
3. The solar plexus chakra
4. The heart chakra
5. The throat chakra
6. The brow chakra—also known as the third eye
7. The crown chakra

Functions and Associations

This is the heart of the chakra method, as it shows us what each chakra is designed to do. Each chakra reflects light and energy, which has its own meaning. The organization works like this:

Flower Images

In addition to the idea of cones or tubes, the chakras can be represented by flower images and there are many of these, depending on which tradition you prefer to use. The Indian tradition uses stylized images of lotus flower petals in the following form:

 The Base (or Root) Chakra symbolizes survival instincts, safety, grounding, and taking nourishment at a basic earth level.

 The Sacral Chakra relates to the emotions, sex, and creativity.

 The Solar Plexus Chakra is linked to willpower, personal power, the mind, and the intellect.

 The Heart Chakra is concerned with compassion, relating to others, and unconditional love.

 The Throat Chakra corresponds to communication, the truth, and creativity.

 The Brow Chakra relates to ESP, inner wisdom, intuition, and psychism.

 The Crown Chakra is associated with spirituality, the universe, and linking with deities and the higher consciousness.

Chakra	Symbol	Number of Petals
Base chakra		four petals
Sacral chakra		six petals
Solar plexus chakra		ten petals
Heart chakra		twelve petals
Throat chakra		sixteen petals
Brow chakra		a petal on each side of a circle
Crown chakra		hundreds of petals

People in the USA or Britain may use different images. Some people use a mental picture of the flowers in place of the cones or tubes, and while purists would say they are wrong, the chakras will still work, however you envisage them. The following is my own take on a system used by some UK spiritualists.

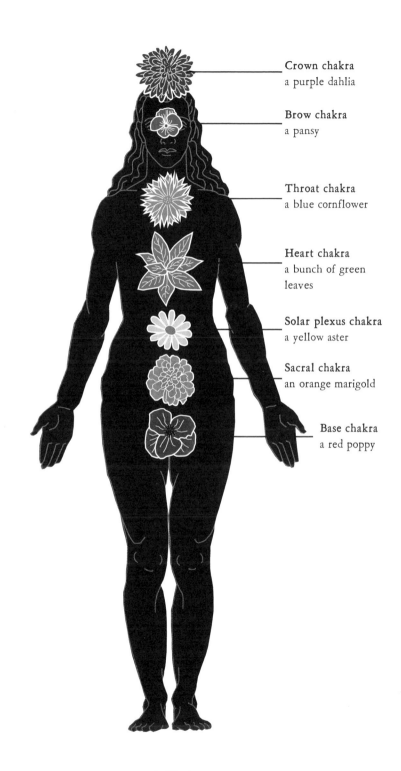

Crown chakra
a purple dahlia

Brow chakra
a pansy

Throat chakra
a blue cornflower

Heart chakra
a bunch of green
leaves

Solar plexus chakra
a yellow aster

Sacral chakra
an orange marigold

Base chakra
a red poppy

Chakras and Colors

The most important thing to grasp is the color system, as it is intrinsic to the chakras. Needless to say, there have been differences of opinion about this over the centuries and there are variations in different parts of the world, but the Western system is based on the colors of the rainbow, with a few additions where required.

Chakra Colors	
	Crown: Purple
	Brow: Indigo
	Throat: Light blue or turquoise
	Heart: Green
	Solar plexus: Yellow
	Sacral: Orange
	Base: Red

Some systems use the seven colors of the rainbow, adding several more chakras rising up from the crown of the head, and these are shown as white.

Kundalini

There is a theory that the seven main chakras are set in motion by an energy source called Kundalini. This energy is supplied by a mystical snake that lies curled up at the bottom of the body by the base of the spine. When activated, the snake uncoils itself and reaches upward, passing one chakra on one side and the following one on the other side, thus using its serpentine body to create a friction that spins the first chakra in one direction and the next in the other direction, and so on. If you like the Kundalini snake image, feel free to use it, but the chakra system works perfectly well if you pay no heed to the notion of Kundalini. As it happens, the chakras are always active, just as the human aura is always on guard, so there is no need to make an effort to set them in motion for normal purposes.

Unusual purposes would include awakening Kundalini to trigger a range of weird experiences that might cause changes in the physical body, the emotional condition, and the psychic ability. The sudden release of energy could cause stress in some areas of the body, or it could open the psyche, heart, and mind to strange visions, shivery feelings, or other odd sensations. It's a good idea to have a knowledgeable person with you if you intend to do any heavy spiritual meditations or rituals designed to work on this kind of intensity.

Kundalini is said to be the force that links us to the earth beneath our feet and the heavens above our heads. It brings sudden enlightenment and can bring feelings of ecstasy of the kind that people experience when performing certain shamanic rituals. It can be activated by doing yoga, by meditating, and, of course, by opening the chakras. You can choose to envisage Kundalini as smoke rising upward from a fire and passing by the revolving drums of the chakras, so if you aren't that keen on the idea of your body being inhabited by a snake, this makes an acceptable substitute.

Astrology

There are seven celestial objects that move across the sky that were known long before telescopes were invented, and these are the sun, moon, Mercury, Venus, Mars, Jupiter, and Saturn. Many different lists have been put forward over the ages to show links between the planets and the chakras, and each has its own convincing explanation. However, here is a commonly understood *modern* link between the chakras and what astrologers call "the planets" meaning the sun, the moon, Mercury, Venus, Mars, Jupiter, and Saturn. The table below shows how the chakras link to the planets and astrological signs.

Chakra	Planet	Connections	Zodiac Signs
Base	Mars	Basic needs	Aries, Scorpio
Sacral	Moon	Relationships	Cancer
Solar plexus	Sun	Energy, will	Leo
Heart	Venus	Unconditional love	Taurus, Libra
Throat	Mercury	Communication	Gemini, Virgo
Brow	Jupiter	Learning, development	Sagittarius, Pisces
Crown	Saturn	Link with the universe	Capricorn, Aquarius

Ancient Associations

Vishnu is associated with the galaxies and the stars, and thus to the study of astronomy and also to the study of astrology. In times gone by, astronomers were also astrologers and vice versa.

Psychology

Each of the seven main chakras is linked to a different aspect of a person's character and personality, so if one chakra becomes weak or damaged, it can upset the others. If a healer treats a misaligned or blocked chakra, this will help all the other chakras and can have a surprisingly beneficial effect on the patient's nature and the way he manages his life.

The Soul

Some traditions say that the soul resides in the crown chakra, but others say it is spread through all the chakras from the solar plexus upward. Whatever the fact of the matter, a blocked chakra will have an effect on the chakras above it.

A Few Warnings

Always have the best of intentions for yourself and for those you wish to heal. Bad wishes will always come back to the person who sent them, and they will probably come back in a worse way than the person intended in the first place.

Don't allow yourself to feel that you are better than other people are, or even that you are better than the person you are healing. When ego appears, spirituality goes out the door, and the healing stops working.

✷ ✷ ✷

2

THE MAJOR CHAKRAS

There are seven major chakras and they line up from the bottom of the spine to the crown of the head, with each chakra running through the body from front to back. Each revolves in a different direction to those above and below it. Some believe there are slight variations on the major chakra theme, whereby some systems divide the heart chakra and brow chakras into two, but we will look into this a little later. The animal totems that you see listed for the chakras are not the same as those in astrology, despite the fact that the planets link with the chakras. For example, the heart chakra is linked to the wolf, but the planet for this chakra is Venus, which astrology associates with the bull.

The Base Chakra

Details
Position: Base of the spine
Main role: Survival, life
Bodily area: Legs, base of the body
Gland: Adrenal
Sense: Smell

Key Ideas
Positive: Security
Negative: Fear, insecurity

Position

The base, or root, chakra is located at the base of the spine, and it tunnels through the body from front to back. In addition to controlling the lower end of the body, it rules the hips, thighs, legs, and feet. Those who work in the spiritual field or who meditate regularly might wish to ground themselves by linking the base chakra to the earth by imagining the spine extending a root downward so that it goes into the earth, or by mentally sending roots down from the soles of the feet.

Base Chakra Topics

This chakra is concerned with the basic needs of food, clothing, and shelter, and it is instinctive—as opposed to emotional, mental, or spiritual—because it is concerned with survival. The base chakra helps to keep us in one piece, so it activates when something or someone threatens our happiness, or even our very survival. For instance, if we find ourselves feeling uncomfortable at the thought of going to a particular place or being in the company of a certain person, the message is coming from the base chakra and it is worth heeding. If you are into palmistry, the base chakra has a connection with the life line and its connection to survival. The base chakra gives us our awareness of the world around us, our place on earth and in society. It rules the need for practical security, and when danger threatens, the adrenaline associated with this chakra kicks in and gives us the instinct for fight or flight.

 The yang, or masculine, aspect of this chakra makes it important where male sexual activity is concerned, especially as the chakra runs through the genital area. It is linked to the warlike planet, Mars, which makes it assertively masculine, but oddly enough, this chakra is also associated with pregnancy and childbirth.

The base chakra relates to the past, our background, our family history and reputation, and our relationship with our mothers. Our childhood experiences, early school life, and early years in general are ruled by the base chakra. This chakra concerns the home, along with safety and seclusion, and it represents a base from which we venture out.

Psychologically, the base chakra refers to events that happened while you were still in the womb and during the first six months of your life. So look back to the events of those times for greater understanding of any problems you may have.

This chakra is the location of the sleeping Kundalini, so its awakening and the start of its upward journey represent the start of the search for the divine.

A Balanced Base Chakra

Here you will find a safe pair of hands that can cope with building, carpentry, electrical and plumbing work, engineering, and gardening. Those with a healthy base chakra have common sense, money in the bank, and a mortgage that they are steadily paying off. This person works hard, and may have the ability to manufacture things or work on products that others want to buy. Alternatively, he could work in a financial field, such as insurance, banking, or

real estate. The base chakra rules the profession and modern concepts of survival that stem from being able to earn a living. In time, it is possible for this person to become wealthy.

Such folk care deeply for their loved ones and they don't desert them easily. If something disastrous happens, the person with a strong base chakra will find a way to get through the situation. Someone of this kind might work in the armed services or as a firefighter, police officer, or security officer. He serves and protects himself, his family, his community, and his country. Hindu tradition says this person will never be in danger from fire.

On a lighter note, this subject loves the countryside and may also be a successful gardener. There is a powerful connection to music and rhythm, especially drumming, so music means a lot to someone with a strong base chakra, as does dancing. He may be into sports and team games, as he is active and strong. He may restrict reading and learning to what he needs for work purposes, so he probably isn't an intellectual. The chakra system connects to ancient astrology and that links the planet Mars to both Aries and Scorpio.

Money, Business, and Career Factors

The primary need for people with a strong base chakra is the need to provide for themselves, because only then can they start to consider the needs of others. These people are good workers and earners, but they can also spend heavily, especially on high-end goods. They might work in engineering, construction, civil engineering, and government projects, or in finance, accountancy, and banking. They read the financial news and keep up to date with politics, economics, and financial matters. These folk can't stand being in debt, and if debt threatens, they have to sort it out quickly or the stress can make them sick.

An Exaggerated Base Chakra

These subjects may be unpleasant themselves, or they may be fine but suffer at the hands of those who are unpleasant, in the forms shown by either the exaggerated or deficient base chakra.

An exaggerated base chakra belongs to someone who is desperate to amass money and possessions, possibly as a hedge against potential future loss and disaster. These people work hard—maybe too hard—and they forget that there are other sides of life, such as family, home life, leisure activities with neighbors and friends, love, relaxation, and spirituality. Sometimes the feeling that life is too difficult can lead the person into addiction to drugs, alcohol, or even food.

Many of the less-attractive personality traits are linked to this chakra, such as materialism, selfishness, cruelty, and a need to exert power over others. There may be racism, a tendency to pick fights, and so on. At heart, these individuals don't think much of themselves, which is why they are so unpleasant to others. They may have a rigid attitude or believe that their own religion is the one that matters, and they may even use religion to exert power over others.

The drive to succeed and to make money can lead to overworking. This can obviously affect these subjects as far as personal relationships go and it can also affect their health.

A Deficient or Damaged Base Chakra

Those with a deficient base chakra lack practicality and common sense and they may be neurotic, nervous, and vulnerable. Others may be so apathetic that they don't get going at all, or if they do, they start something but never finish it.

Damage to the base chakra occurs when the really big events of life come along and threaten our very existence. The biggest events are the apocalyptic ones of war, pestilence, famine, and death, but in our modern world, the big events might be sickness or death of a family member, a life-changing accident, or a life-threatening health diagnosis. Events such as the breakup of a relationship, the loss of a home, a business going under, and severe financial problems will also weaken and unbalance the base chakra, so healing to this chakra might be just the thing to help someone cope.

There may be problems related to sex that lead to impotence, which in turn can lead to anger and frustration.

Body and Health

Legend has it that a problem with the left hip, leg, or foot signals a difficult relationship with the mother, whereas a problem with the right hip, leg, or foot suggests a difficult relationship with the father. Such relationship problems may have happened in the past or they may be ongoing.

Common base chakra complaints are back pain, especially sciatica that travels down the leg, apathy and lethargy, feeling cold, and not wanting to move about much. This chakra is also said to represent the skeletal system, so arthritis and dental problems may occur. There may be bowel or digestive problems, but the base chakra also rules unhealthy eating patterns, such as overeating, bulimia, and anorexia. Blood pressure may also be an issue.

- Cervical erosion
- Thrush
- Cystitis
- Venereal diseases
- Hemorrhoids
- Anal fistulas
- Prostate problems
- Testicular problems
- Sterility
- Impotence
- Incontinence
- Vaginal problems
- AIDS

- Constipation
- Diarrhea
- Sciatica
- High or low blood pressure
- Arthritis
- Dental problems
- Sinus and other nasal problems
- Cancer
- Anorexia
- Bulimia
- Overeating
- Addictions

Correspondences

The corresponding ideas listed below are linked to the base chakra. Some of these items come into their own when we apply complementary therapies or energy healing.

Vedic name:	Muladhara
Other names:	Root chakra, red chakra
Number:	The first chakra
Color:	Red
Gender:	Yang, masculine, positive
Animal:	Elephant
Lotus petals:	Four
Shape:	Square
Element:	Earth
Planet:	Mars
Zodiac signs:	Aires and Scorpio
Mantra:	Lam
Music:	Drumming

The Sacral Chakra

Details
Position: Abdomen through to the sacral spine
Main role: Creation, emotions
Bodily areas: Reproductive organs, bowels
Glands: Ovaries, testes
Sense: Taste

Key Ideas
Positive: Values self
Negative: Has low self-esteem

Position
The site of the sacral chakra is the abdomen, and the back of it connects with the lumbar and sacral spine, the sciatic nerve, and the pelvis. It is concerned with the reproductive system, especially the ovaries and testes.

Sacral Chakra Topics
Like the base chakra, this is an instinctual chakra, but it also concerns the emotions—and strong emotions at that. It relates to both sharing and independence, with joining and separating, and with shared resources and separate ones. If you are into astrology, the sacral chakra is linked to the moon and the sign of cancer. Since this chakra is linked to the moon, it tends to *react* to circumstances and suffer as a result of them rather than cause them. If you are into palmistry, it can be worth checking out the start of the life line, where

it is close to the head line, and, conversely, the lower end of the life line and its connection to the fate line. These line positions talk about family, school friends, and love relationships we have in early life and the effect they have on us in adulthood.

The sacral chakra rules love, sex, attachment to others, and important relationships, so it is the site of many emotions. There is a real urge to help others and to put the world right, but a person with a strong sacral chakra can attract lame ducks, so he must try to hold back when others attempt to lean on him. Fortunately, there is a level of intuition associated with self-preservation, so if the subject feels that someone wishes to take advantage of him, he is probably right. The ideal situation is to give and take, but neither to lean too much on others nor to allow others to lean too heavily on him.

The sacral chakra is said to be formed between the ages of six months and two-and-a-half years, so events that occur at that time will have a profound influence on the individual in adulthood.

A Balanced Sacral Chakra

The sacral chakra is considered to be the largest of the chakras, so when we feel scared or upset our bowels can feel as though they have turned to water and we can also have an urgent need to empty our bladders. While the majority of matters related to the basics of survival are linked to the base chakra, this chakra still has some survival concerns, although there is more interest in interaction with others than is the case with the "self-interested" base chakra.

One of the sacral chakra's main concerns is sex—along with attraction and intimate relationships—so this chakra brings people together. The sacral chakra is also associated with creativity, and this extends to creating a family, so sex, love, and procreation are part of the picture here. The motherly nature of this chakra can lead these subjects to choose a profession that involves caring for young people.

This chakra is too low on the scale to allow for logic or intellect, but there is "gut feeling" and intuition here, and this helps these subjects to know what's best for them, so they usually know whom they can trust and who is likely to do them harm. These people are similar to those who have a strong moon on their astrological chart, which makes them sensitive to what is going on in their bodies. They are usually the first to know if something is going wrong. They are also acutely aware of the moods and illnesses of those they care about, and they even know when a pet is coming down with an ailment.

Those with a strong sacral chakra exert control over their own emotions and behavior, so they make pleasant friends, relatives, and neighbors. They work well with others and make the best of things, and while they feel good about themselves, they are rarely arrogant. They won't allow others to rule them and they don't become victims. They set rules for their children and loved ones, and make such sacrifices as are relevant to their family situation. They enjoy the good things of life but accept that a little rain must fall from time to time. They are content, sensible, and reasonable.

The sacral chakra is linked to the person's past, the family background, and roots, but while the past can be harmful to some, when the chakra is balanced, the past exerts a healthy influence. These subjects may do things the way their parents did or they may find another way of doing things, but they are proud of their background and keep in touch with their families.

People who are into the spiritual world would make good healers, because there is an element of clairsentience here, suggesting the ability to "feel" someone's bodily and emotional pain and to give the kind of healing that would ease it.

Money, Business, and Career Factors

These people are sensitive, sensual, and creative. They have strong feelings about what appeals to the senses and the look and feel of things are more important than what they cost. These individuals may work in the field of fashion design, cosmetics, beauty therapy, and alternative therapies, such as aromatherapy or reflexology. They also make good counselors because they like to help others, but they have to walk the fine line between being compassionate and being used. They are most likely to be successful when they are happy.

Those who have a strong sacral chakra are not in love with money but they appreciate the freedom that it confers. These folks can succeed in business by creating goods that others want to buy, and they take pleasure from the creative process of building a business. Their intuitive understanding of other people makes them excellent employers and fine salespeople. They are sociable and somewhat ambitious, although not necessarily money-minded as they prefer to be part of a collective situation where pulling together is needed. An attraction to water can lead them to careers on the sea, such as on cruise liners or in the fishing industry, or they might even clean and repair swimming pools.

Their personal finances may be chaotic, and they can lose out by forgetting to attend to bank and credit card statements. Where health is concerned, it's unlikely that money problems would make them sick, but if the problems stem from the breakup of a relationship, the emotional upheaval would definitely have an effect.

An Exaggerated Sacral Chakra

The subjects may be unpleasant themselves, or they may be fine but suffer at the hands of those who are unpleasant, in the forms shown by either the exaggerated or deficient sacral chakra.

Emotions run wild when this chakra is out of sorts, so this can lead to obsessing over someone who doesn't return the person's love or there may be fights over finances, sex, infidelity, love triangles, and so on. Jealousy, bullying or being bullied, violence, and noisy outbursts can occur, which makes family life deeply unpleasant for all concerned. All of this can lead to addiction to food, drink, or drugs.

A Deficient Sacral Chakra

Those who have a weak or unbalanced sacral chakra may be nervous, afraid, and vulnerable, and they may avoid getting involved with others for fear of being hurt. This may be a temporary situation due to trauma and emotional pain, but it could come from being put down by others or used by them for their own benefit. Some sacral chakra types are calculating by nature, and thus unattractive to potential lovers, or they are so taken up with their work or their interests, they don't want or need love or family life. Sometimes a person with a weak sacral chakra can be so busy doing things for others that they put their own needs last and lose touch with their own likes and dislikes. Some prefer the company of animals to people, and that is fine if they are happy that way.

If you are normally well balanced but are in a temporary state of discontent or sadness, you may need to talk things over with a good friend. If you are very upset, perhaps book a session with a life coach or a psychotherapist.

Body and Health

Just as the moon in astrology is concerned with moodiness, restlessness, and changeability, so is the sacral chakra. The tendency to mess up relationships can lead to loneliness, sadness, and a lack of love, all of which leads to depression. Fertility is ruled by this chakra, so many sacral chakra ailments are the same as those ruled by the base chakra.

Some say that this chakra rules the female reproductive organs in women and the spleen in men. In women, the chakra is connected to the monthly cycle and to the condition of the uterus and ovaries. While such problems can cause mood swings in women, in both sexes, such ailments as lumbago, slipped discs, sciatica, and so on make the sufferer understandably bad tempered.

This chakra is particularly concerned with nutrition and digestion, so it relates to eating problems, and it may be that these people should restrict carbohydrates and eat lots of fresh vegetables, fruits, and salads.

Here is a list of ailments that can be linked to the sacral chakra:

- Cervical erosion
- Thrush
- Cystitis
- Candida
- Prostate problems
- Testicular problems
- Sterility
- Impotence
- Incontinence
- Vaginal problems

- AIDS
- Sciatica
- Slipped disc
- Lumbago
- Asthma
- Eczema
- Anorexia
- Bulimia
- Overeating

Correspondences

The corresponding ideas listed below are linked to the sacral chakra. Some of these items come into their own when we apply complementary therapies or energy healing.

Vedic name:	Svadhistana
Other names:	Spleen chakra, orange chakra
Number:	The second chakra
Color:	Orange
Gender:	Yin, feminine, negative
Animal:	Crocodile
Lotus petals:	Six
Shape:	Crescent moon, pyramid
Element:	Water
Planet:	Moon
Zodiac sign:	Cancer
Mantra:	Vam
Music:	Strings

The Solar Plexus Chakra

Details

Position: Above the naval through to central spine
Main role: Energy, control, and belief
Bodily area: Digestion
Glands: Pancreas, endocrine
Sense: Sight

Key Ideas

Positive: Good use of willpower
Negative: Others walk over the subject

Position

The solar plexus chakra is just above the naval and extends through to the central spine.

Solar Plexus Chakra Topics

Tradition says the solar plexus chakra is the first of the *emotional* chakras rather than being one that is instinctive, mental, or spiritual, yet it is mainly concerned with thought, ideas, and the conveyance of information. It is the perfect chakra for the modern world, especially for those in middle management who are climbing the corporate ladder. This is the chakra of intelligence, technology, science, and success in our robotic and computerized age. It specifically rules the obtaining of information through education, reading, television, and the internet, but it then rules the ability to give that information out again, as in teaching, giving presentations, and via blogs, articles, and books. It rules curiosity and the need to know and to learn.

The solar plexus chakra is associated with focusing on ideas, goals, ambitions, and on having the determination, courage, and confidence to go after these things. From an astrological point of view, this chakra has the targeted aim of the tenth house, along with the organizational ability of Leo and the love of information that links with Gemini. The solar plexus chakra is about leadership and the ability to direct and control others in a managerial role, but both control and self-control are ruled by this chakra, along with the amount of leeway that individuals allow themselves or give to others.

Tradition says the solar plexus chakra was formed between the ages of two-and-a-half and four-and-a-half, so events that occurred at that time will have a profound effect on the individual in adulthood.

A Balanced Solar Plexus Chakra

Combine the career success associated with the solar plexus chakra with happy relationships, good friendships, good health, an active mind, money to spare, interesting pastimes, and the ability to relax and enjoy a holiday every now and again—and we have the very definition of a successful person. However, this chakra is also about feelings of self-worth and self-confidence, and those come from within. A successful person has a definite purpose in life and a fair chance of achieving his or her aims. When the solar plexus chakra is working properly, it gives the person energy, willpower, and the confidence and courage to grasp new ideas and initiatives and to tackle new projects and see them through to the finish.

These people don't allow others to push them around, but they aren't aggressive or unpleasant. They can help others and put themselves out for family and friends, but they aren't self-sacrificial nor do they become victims. They don't worry unnecessarily, and they aren't neurotic or fearful, so they are confident, cheerful, and normally both healthy and happy. However, even those with well-balanced solar plexus chakras can fail in their love relationships, because they may be too busy achieving success in their careers to give the time, attention, and love needed to make a partnership work.

Those who have a strong solar plexus chakra would make excellent spiritual healers, as they can tap into the bodily and emotional pain of others, and give healing in order to make the sick or unhappy person feel better.

Money, Business, and Career Factors

The desire to gather information puts these people in front in our modern world, but they would have been equally at home several hundred years ago, working out accounts with a quill pen and an abacus! Budgeting comes naturally to them, and the logic of accounts suits their mind-set. They need a goal to work toward and they work hard to achieve it. If they have to fight their corner in business, like a good lawyer, they don't go into battle without gathering all the data they can beforehand.

Reputation is more important to these individuals than money, so they might move up the political ladder or work their way up the service ladder to become senior police officers or firefighters or military officers. They enjoy wielding power over others, and they certainly like to be respected, but they also have a creative streak that leads them to enjoy the process of making something or building an enterprise, and a good result means a lot to them.

An Exaggerated Solar Plexus Chakra

The subjects may be unpleasant themselves, or they may be fine but suffer at the hands of those who are unpleasant, in the forms shown by either the exaggerated or deficient solar plexus chakra.

These individuals can be talented computer programmers or analysts. Computers don't have emotions, so machinery of this kind suits their cold manner and logical, analytical style. They may be like an unpleasant version of a Star Trek Vulcan.

They may enjoy arguing or take pleasure in freezing out their partners with long silences, which makes the partners feel lonely and unappreciated. Just about every unpleasant behavior pattern can display itself, such as anger, bullying, irritability, sarcasm, destructive hurtfulness, and so on. Some of these subjects are fusspots who make an issue over silly things, imposing stupid rules on others while allowing themselves to do as they please. If in the right mood, these folk can be witty and amusing, but nobody can stand to have them in their homes, offices, and lives for long. Yet they fear being alone, so they look for ways to be with others.

A Deficient Solar Plexus Chakra

These individuals can be desperate for understanding, approval, acceptance, and love. They are people-pleasers who give way to others and sacrifice far too much, but they aren't thanked for all their good deeds. They are insecure and short of confidence, so it is hard for them to achieve anything. They may be lethargic, lacking in intelligence, and pessimistic, and may make bad decisions or wrong choices. They can't raise the energy to be passionate about anything, so they don't achieve much. They are self-effacing and indecisive, and can be overwhelmed by their emotions or even hormonal imbalances, which allows others to take advantage of them for their own benefit.

Some of these individuals can make a success of themselves in work or in some kind of organization, but their "success" may come about in a roundabout or underhanded way. Such people may actually think a lot of themselves, when there is nothing special about them.

Sometimes their sad situation comes about due to them being sick, or being stuck at home for some reason, perhaps caring for a number of children or nursing a sick relative, which makes it impossible to keep a job or pursue a hobby. Some become weak due to age, and there is little that can be done to help them at this stage.

Body and Health

This chakra is in the middle of the body, so it rules the organs of digestion. If the chakra is in trouble, there may be difficulty digesting food or converting it into energy. This results in malnutrition, fatigue, and poor recuperative powers. It relates badly when the subject feels under attack, so unpleasant circumstances or 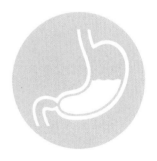 continuous arguments or being on the receiving end of constant bullying will cause the main organs of the body to fall prey to diseases, possibly even cancer.

Ailments that can be attributed to the solar plexus chakra are:

- Stomach ulcers
- Gastric blockages
- Liver problems
- Pancreatic problems
- Gallstones
- Diabetes
- Hypoglycemia
- Weight gain
- Problems with the adrenal glands
- Kidney problems
- Parasitic diseases
- Malaria
- Skin problems
- Eye problems

Correspondences

The corresponding ideas listed below are linked to the solar plexus chakra. Some of these items come into their own when we apply complementary therapies or energy healing.

Vedic name:	Manipura
Other names:	Yellow chakra, naval chakra
Number:	The third chakra
Color:	Yellow
Gender:	Yang, masculine, positive
Animal:	Ram
Lotus petals:	Ten
Shape:	Circle
Element:	Fire
Planet:	Sun
Zodiac sign:	Leo
Mantra:	Ram
Music:	Reed and horn

The Heart Chakra

Details

Position: Central chest through to the spine
Main role: Love, relating, respect, and creativity
Bodily areas: Heart, lungs, and upper digestive tract
Gland: Thymus
Sense: Touch

Key Ideas

Positive: Loving and loved, compassionate
Negative: Unloving or unloved

Position

The heart chakra goes through the chest and heart and out through the spine.

Heart Chakra Topics

This is the second of the *emotional* chakras, as opposed to the base and sacral chakras—called the *instinctual* chakras—and the throat and brow chakras, which are the *intelligence* chakras, or the crown and further chakras, which are *spiritual* chakras. The heart chakra is the doorway between the survival-oriented lower chakras and the spiritually-oriented upper ones.

Old-fashioned poems and modern pop songs tell us that the heart is activated when people fall in love, and even more so when something goes badly wrong. After all, we talk about heartbreak when we lose someone we love. If you are into palmistry, you may know that the heart line shows both the health of the heart as an organ and the story of the person's love life. For instance, a broken heart line does tell of a broken heart, but the line can show recovery and new love interests coming along later. So the heart chakra is all about love in all its forms and the ability to relate to others. This chakra is also concerned with emotional security and with the certainty of being loved by others. It seeks to form a balance between the need for love and the desire for spiritual excellence, so it rules selflessness, compassion, devotion, and a reasonable measure of sacrifice on behalf of others.

The heart chakra also relates to the good things of life, such as creativity and pleasure from art, music, and dance, and it even connects with craftwork and creating a lovely home or garden. So this links with physical and emotional healing on one hand but also with fun, amusement, and upliftment, in addition to relaxation, rest, and recovery.

If you like astrology, this chakra links with the sign of Libra, which is associated with partnerships and relationships between people. It also relates to events that occurred between the ages of four-and-a-half and six-and-a-half years old, so you should look back to your life at that age to see how it has subsequently affected you.

A Balanced Heart Chakra

People who have a strong heart chakra are comfortable with themselves, so while they know they aren't perfect, they also know they are on the right track. They don't worry about little things, but they do try to put things right when big things go wrong. These people are kind, loving, and unselfish, but they don't allow themselves to become martyrs or to be used and manipulated by others. They are sincere and honest in their behavior toward others, and they are happy to love others but need to be loved in return. They can live with themselves if they make a mistake and they don't expect others to be perfect either, so their attitude is generally sensible and reasonable.

Those who have a strong heart chakra are easy enough to live with, to work alongside, and to be around, because they have a healthy dose of self-respect and also gain the respect of others. Even if they decide to put their own life on hold to take care of others, this is something they choose to do rather than something imposed on them. Some of these individuals are so charitable that they work for the benefit of others. They trust others unless they find a good reason not to do so. Some turn to religion or spirituality either as part of their life or by working in the religious arena.

They are not cold or unemotional, but they don't fall into a heap of self-pity or dejection when things go wrong. They understand that even bad times are necessary for growth, but generally speaking, they hope for the best.

These individuals can handle loss, separation, bereavement, and heartache with a degree of equilibrium and acceptance. Their main drive is love, compassion, and kindness, but they aren't fools or victims, so if someone seeks to take advantage of them, they walk away from the situation.

Money, Business, and Career Factors

Those with a strong heart chakra neither hoard money nor waste it, and they are neither tight fisted nor overgenerous, so while they don't worship money or goods, they ensure that they and their loved ones have enough for a comfortable lifestyle. Those who are influenced by their heart chakra work with people in careers that require teamwork, so they can be found in the armed services, law enforcement, schools, hospitals, ambulance service, and so on. If the job helps the public, so much the better, which means they can be found helping the elderly, disabled, underprivileged, and children. If they can't find jobs in these fields, they will be scout leaders, volunteers who help homeless or addicted people, and so on.

Those who have a strong heart chakra might work as psychic counselors, tarot readers, healers, and spiritual advisors, due to their ability to tap into the emotional needs of others.

An Exaggerated Heart Chakra

These subjects may be unpleasant themselves, or they may be fine but suffer at the hands of those who are unpleasant, in the forms shown by either the exaggerated or deficient heart chakra.

In most cases, an overactive heart chakra isn't a bad thing as far as other people are concerned, but it is wearing and damaging for the individuals who have this issue. Too much heart chakra can make these people too sacrificial, too ready to give their money or possessions away, too quick to help others, and too inclined to "rescue" a very needy partner, or perhaps one who is an alcoholic or a drug addict. They put the needs of others above their own needs, and their loyalty and love are misplaced.

This chakra is a problem in those who seek to push others around by emotional means, so they enjoy upsetting everyone by making loud and emotional scenes, such as on their phones or social media, telling their friends and colleagues how badly they are being treated—while it is often they themselves who are causing at least half the trouble. They may give love only when something is likely to come their way as a result, so they make nightmarish parents and impossible partners. They encourage a child to believe in them, and then turn on the child. They enjoy exerting power over others and exploit those who rely on them at work, in the home, and elsewhere. They can be manipulative bullies who pose as victims. They are bitter and full of spleen, and they cannot forgive and forget.

The individual may suffer from jealousy, even to the extent of wanting to hurt others because they are luckier or better off than he is, yet the person won't do anything to change his situation or improve his life.

A Deficient Heart Chakra

Some people do too much for others in the hopes of receiving love, understanding, and approval in return. They love to make others happy, but forget that they are also entitled to happiness. If they play the martyr, they can be tiring and wearing, as they lean on others and drain them. Some individuals confuse love with money and give far too much of their income away in the hopes of being loved in return. Sadly, sometimes they do this just for the sake of peace rather than in any expectation of being truly loved.

Situations that involve relating to others require courage, common sense, and the ability to set limits—and this applies to colleagues and bosses at work and to family members—so while those with a weak heart chakra might be put upon, they allow this to happen rather than standing up for themselves. They may live in a toxic situation, among people who should love and care for them but don't, and this affects their self-worth and self-confidence to the point where they feel stupid and worthless. They may feel unworthy of being on the receiving end of love, approval, respect, or decent behavior. They may feel ill equipped to deal with anything.

In some cases, those with a deficient heart chakra may be happy in their own company, fond of animals, or get a lot of pleasure out of creating a lovely garden or painting, singing, or doing something else artistic and creative. They may not wish to be part of a partnership or to work with others. These people are self-sufficient and happy to do their own thing their own way.

Body and Health

The heart is ruled by this chakra but also everything in the chest area, including the lungs, ribs, upper spine, and shoulders. The list below shows the bodily areas and functions associated with this chakra.

- Heart
- Lungs
- Circulation
- Rib cage
- Upper spine
- Shoulders
- Blood cells
- Thymus
- Growth hormones
- Digestive tract
- Upper stomach

This list shows the ailments associated with the heart chakra:

- Asthma
- Allergies
- Pneumonia
- Emphysema
- Arthritis in spine and shoulders
- Hiatus hernia
- Problems related to the breasts
- Cancer of the lungs or the breasts

Correspondences

The corresponding ideas listed below are linked to the heart chakra. Some of these items come into their own when we apply complementary therapies or energy healing.

Vedic name:	Anahata
Other name:	Green chakra
Number:	The fourth chakra
Color:	Green
Gender:	Yin, feminine, negative
Animal:	Wolf
Lotus petals:	Twelve
Shape:	Cross
Element:	Air
Planet:	Venus
Zodiac signs:	Taurus and Libra
Mantra:	Yam
Music:	Flute, woodwind instruments

The Throat Chakra

Details

Position: The throat through to the nape of the neck

Main role: Communication

Bodily area: Throat

Glands: Thyroid and parathyroid

Sense: Hearing

Key Ideas

Positive: Clarity of expression

Negative: Lies and obfuscation

Position

This chakra is at the throat at the front and the nape of the neck at the back. It rules the neck, upper shoulders, upper spine, bronchial system, speech, hearing, jaws, and the thyroid and parathyroid glands.

Throat Chakra Topics

This is the chakra of the intellect, as opposed to the instinctual, emotional, or spiritual chakras, so it is associated with logic, reason, and common sense. This chakra is associated with learning and teaching, and with taking in knowledge and communicating it to others. It can rule artistic interests, especially music and poetry. It rules listening to a teacher, along with education through reading and watching educational programs on television. It is the chakra of communication that is involved with listening, talking, writing, and connecting with others for both business and personal purposes. It is also the chakra that rules the development of character and personal strength through experience and the ability to earn a decent living and care for others. It refers to common sense, understanding, and responsibility, including being responsible for oneself.

As far as health is concerned, this chakra is associated with growth and the development of the hormones. Psychologically, this chakra is said to hark back to the things that happened to the person between the ages of six-and-a-half and eight-and-a-half, so experiences that occurred then will have a profound effect on the individual in adulthood.

If you are into astrology, this chakra links with the planet Mercury and the air signs of Gemini, Libra, and Aquarius. Gemini is the sign most concerned with communication, while both Libra and Aquarius have a strong sense of justice and a desire to make the world a better place for humankind, and this links squarely with the nature of this chakra.

Some traditions see this chakra as a "filter" that keeps the mundane world away from the spiritual world, which is the focus of the upper chakras.

A Balanced Throat Chakra

People with a strong throat chakra take responsibility for their actions and don't look around for people to blame when they make mistakes. They take credit for their own achievements and accept their own shortcomings, so in this way they earn the respect of others. They are loyal, decent, trustworthy, and honest, and while also diplomatic and tactful, they aren't stupid, so they quickly see through the machinations of others.

Those with a strong throat chakra rarely lean on others in the worldly sense, but they have a strong spiritual belief, so if life becomes difficult, they can turn to their beliefs and know they will receive the help they need. They do the right thing for the right reason, so there is an underlying spirituality here and an unconscious spiritual attitude to everything they do—they try to be honest and decent and charitable toward others. These people are really good listeners, so they learn to understand the position of others and to empathize with them.

Money, Business, and Career Factors

People with a strong throat chakra make good counselors, but they can also work in the legal sphere or in local or national politics. They can be good orators and are drawn to writing, publishing, journalism, and broadcasting. They may design computer programs and software for games and entertainment or for educational purposes. These people are excellent in business and have a knack for understanding the corporate world. They might work in accountancy or banking, because they understand finances, but they also enjoy advising and helping other people.

These individuals take personal responsibility for their decisions, set realistic goals, and get things done. They succeed in the material world and lead fulfilling lives. However, when things don't work out, they are able to accept what cannot be. They are realistic. Because they negotiate well, they can be excellent salespeople. A well-balanced throat chakra encourages individuals to stretch themselves, to accept challenges and to aim high. These people can visualize their future and work toward it, because they are good planners, but they may be less able to deal with details.

Some people are so desperate to communicate that they talk too much and bore others, or they give away too much information. Sometimes this is the result of being nervous, but in other cases, the person just likes the sound of their own voice. In business, it is better to listen than to talk, and those with a well-balanced and clear throat chakra understand this well.

If these people choose to work part-time or full-time in the psychic field, they can be clairaudient, which means they can hear the voices of those who have passed over. Some can tune in to the words of spiritual guides and even those of the angelic realm. They can help others by listening to them and by giving therapy, counseling, or help during traumatic times.

An Exaggerated Throat Chakra

These subjects may be unpleasant themselves, or they may be fine but suffer at the hands of those who are unpleasant, in the forms shown by either the exaggerated or deficient throat chakra.

There are people who are so fond of themselves and their own opinions that they make life difficult for those around them. They may be religious or politically dogmatic, and it's likely that the only things that matter to them are their own prejudices. They can't understand others or empathize with others, but then, they don't care about others. These intolerant folk blame everyone else for their own mistakes and shortcomings, and they don't take personal responsibility for their errors. They may be mouthy, arrogant, and boring, or they may be waspish, spiteful, self-righteous know-it-alls or just plain stupid. They lack courage and verve; they avoid effort, taking the best jobs and the best of everything on offer, without sharing with or caring about others. They are jealous of others and spiteful toward them. They enjoy life only when pushing others around.

A Deficient Throat Chakra

Pessimistic, melancholic, and lacking in courage, but like weak people the world over, they can be devious and able to slide out of doing anything useful. They look back in bitterness and harbor grudges, blaming others for all that is wrong in their lives. They find it hard to stick up for themselves, so they turn to strong people and lean on them, sometimes ending up being around bullies who take advantage of them. Other people's opinions may have too large a place in the subject's life.

They do all they can to placate others and to avoid generating anger in others, so they may give money or goods away to buy a little peace and quiet. Many of these people find themselves stuck in bad relationships, and those with a weak throat chakra find it impossible to speak out about the injustices they suffer. Alternatively, they do speak out but nobody wants to listen to them. They can put up with difficult relationships or impossible situations for years before they decide to strike out on their own. Some take the blame for things that have nothing to do with them, and others who should leave a bad situation stay put in the hopes that it will eventually improve.

Body and Health

Obviously, this chakra is associated with the throat, but also with the cervical spine, shoulders, and upper part of the body. Here are the ailments that are associated with the throat chakra:

- Bronchitis
- Asthma
- Laryngitis
- Tonsillitis
- Allergies
- Vocal chord problems
- Mouth ulcers
- Dental problems
- Anorexia and bulimia
- Neck and cervical spine conditions
- Problems with growth and development
- Thyroid and parathyroid ailments
- Hearing and balance problems
- Menstrual cycle and menopausal problems

Correspondences

The corresponding ideas listed below are linked to the throat chakra. Some of these items come into their own when we apply complementary therapies or energy healing.

Vedic name:	Vishuddha
Other name:	Light blue chakra
Number:	The fifth chakra
Color:	Sky blue
Gender:	Yang, masculine, positive
Animal:	Eagle
Lotus petals:	Sixteen
Shape:	Cup
Element:	Air/Ether
Planet:	Mercury
Zodiac signs:	Gemini and Virgo
Facial Area:	Throat
Mantra:	Ham
Music:	Singing

The Brow Chakra

Details

Position: Central forehead just above the eyes
Main role: Knowledge, clarity
Bodily area: Head
Gland: Pineal/pituitary
Sense: Sight

Key Ideas

Positive: Insight
Negative: Muddled thinking

Position

This chakra is often called the *third eye*. Some say that it is located between the eyes, while others believe that it sits in the center of the forehead.

Brow Chakra Topics

The brow chakra really kicks in when we work in a spiritual manner, whether as mediums, psychics, or healers. The chakra rules extrasensory perception and the ability to connect with discarnate entities. It is also associated with psychology, in the sense of being able to understand others and ourselves. This chakra rules emotional intelligence and maturity, and it can help individuals to see what's behind the actions of others as well as their own. It brings the gifts of intuition and inspiration and the ability to access messages from the spirit world. It is especially connected to clairvoyance and second sight.

A Balanced Brow Chakra

Now we start to move away from daily life, as this is the first of the spiritual chakras. The brow chakra also rules thinking, imagination, and creativity, in that it helps individuals to bring their ideas to life. It is the sign of the visionary. This chakra is also linked to memory, so it allows people to learn from past mistakes and past hurts, and to move toward something better in the future. Tradition links this chakra to the relationship with the mother and to the person's feelings about his or her mother, so there is that link to the past, along with a vision of the long-term future. Another link to the past is the age group that this chakra is said to relate back to, which is eight-and-a-half to ten-and-a-half.

This chakra helps subjects to be decent, honest, loyal, reliable, and sympathetic. These people are sensible and open minded but also clear sighted and earnest. They take responsibility for themselves, but also do all they can to help others. They use their strength in a positive way, often to make the planet and all that is on it and in it a better place. This chakra forms a bridge between the mundane world and the world of spirit. Astrologically speaking, the planet Jupiter and the signs of Sagittarius and Pisces seem to link to this chakra.

This is the chakra of clairvoyance, which is the ability to see spirit or to receive psychic and spiritual visions. It is adept at interpreting symbols that the person receives in dreams or during spiritual work. It is linked to such things as oracle cards and the tarot because of its ability to translate images into messages. The insight that this chakra endows will allow individuals to see through lies and subterfuge and to get to the truth of the matter.

Money, Business, and Career Factors

A job is a job but business requires vision, so this chakra, which is so involved in spiritual work, can also aid those who want to make big bucks in business. The generous nature of the chakra means that once these people have made some money, they give freely to their loved ones and to some kind of cause. Where a job or career is concerned, these visionary people should use their talents in architecture, local or national government, the law, insurance, or retirement planning—they are long-term planners. If they decide to put on an event that helps others or makes the world a better place, it will succeed.

There is a symbolic idea that connects to routes, roadways, and pathways here, so someone with a strong brow chakra can find a way through a dilemma or a route or pathway that leads from one situation to another.

On a practical note, this can mean a career in long-term visionary work, such as town planning or civil engineering. If you have a strong brow chakra, be sure to arrange a good retirement plan for yourself and you'll do your best to pay off your mortgage.

Money doesn't rule these people, so many are attracted to creative pursuits or spiritual work. Some work as clairvoyants, spiritual healers, mediums, and so on.

An Exaggerated Brow Chakra

The subjects may be unpleasant themselves, or they may be fine but suffer at the hands of those who are unpleasant, in the forms shown by either the exaggerated or deficient brow chakra.

People with an exaggerated brow chakra are bossy, unpleasant, arrogant, and egotistical, with no reason other than their own high opinion of themselves. They love themselves while behaving badly toward others. They may be stubborn and unbending with closed minds and no imagination, and they may ridicule those around them. They certainly don't concern themselves with the needs of others.

They bore others by going on about their own interests, and this can be the case for spiritually minded people as much as it is for anyone else. In palmistry, those who have a short head line are like this, as they know all there is to know about one topic, and the only way to get through to them is by talking about it. They are the train-spotters and pigeon fanciers of the world. Some may be misogynistic, anti-Semitic, and racist, and strangely, this kind of bully can also be extremely religious and a pillar of his or her church. Sometimes it is the ideas of other people that have too much influence on this person, and he finds himself in trouble as a result.

A Deficient Brow Chakra

Although not short of intuition, these people find it hard to get down to anything, so they never manage to finish what they start or to gain much in the way of self-esteem. They sacrifice too much to others in the hopes of keeping the peace, but it doesn't really work. They can't stand up for themselves. There is a fine line between admiration and envy, and those with such low self-esteem tend to envy others. They are easily upset and they are sensitive, overanalyzing painful situations and finding it hard to cope with criticism or move on after put-downs. They suffer in childhood, possibly due to a lack of love and then later in life by living and working alongside difficult people. Needless to say, some turn to alcohol or other drugs to numb the pain. They can end up being lonely and isolated, but some prefer this to the company of others, and if these folks get a pet to love and care for, this can save their sanity and perhaps even their lives.

Body and Health

This chakra rules the head, but also several glands around the body. It is connected to hormones that relate to female problems and it has some connection to sleeplessness. The ailments associated with this chakra are:

- Headaches
- Migraine
- Neuralgia
- Sinusitis
- Giddiness
- Sleeplessness
- Hormone imbalances
- Vision problems, including blindness
- Brain tumors
- Strokes
- Brain hemorrhage
- Spinal problems
- Balance, movement, and coordination problems
- Pineal and pituitary gland problems

Correspondences

The corresponding ideas listed below are linked to the brow chakra. Some of these items come into their own when we apply complementary therapies or energy healing

Vedic name:	Ajna
Other names:	Third eye chakra, frontal chakra, indigo chakra
Number:	The sixth chakra
Color:	Indigo blue
Gender:	Yang, masculine, positive
Animal:	Ancestors
Lotus petals:	A circle with a petal on each side
Shape:	Star of David
Element:	Light
Planet:	Jupiter
Zodiac signs:	Sagittarius and Pisces
Facial Area:	Eyes, skull
Mantra:	Aum
Music:	Sacred songs and music

The Crown Chakra

Details

Position: The crown of the head
Main role: Spirituality
Bodily areas: Head and central nervous system
Gland: Pineal/pituitary
Sense: Oneness with the universe

Key Ideas

Positive: Spirituality
Negative: Cannot be trusted

Position

The crown chakra is located on the crown of the head.

Crown Chakra Topics

This chakra links human beings to both the earth and the universe. It rules spirituality, brotherhood, and faith. This chakra contains memories of past lives and glimpses of the next life. It is the gateway to the higher consciousness, spirituality, guided intuition, and an understanding of the real meaning of life and the afterlife. The crown chakra rules faith, trust, prayer, meditation, and wisdom, but it also links to happiness and joy.

A Balanced Crown Chakra

Those who have a well-balanced and strong crown chakra love and understand people, so they might choose to work for the benefit of humankind and for the glory of God. They are generous and intelligent. Subjects with a healthy crown chakra understand their purpose on earth, and they have a good idea of how they want to live and what they want to achieve.

Oddly enough, feelings of fear, loneliness, isolation, and bereavement can be linked to this chakra even when it is properly aligned. Some form of intense suffering can lead people to search for answers and to find spirituality, and this may eventually guide them to comfort and counsel others.

Money, Business, and Career Factors

Those with a well-aligned crown chakra have values that are spiritual rather than material, so they may work in selfless careers, such as helping addicts and the homeless, or caring for those who are less fortunate than they are. In some cases, these individuals choose to become ministers of religion or even monks and nuns. Many aren't interested in money at all, but feel their job is to bring the word and love of God to others.

Those who work in the commercial world are ethical and always try to do a good day's work in exchange for a good day's pay. If they sell something or perform a service, they need to feel that it is of benefit to others. They are honest and decent, and prefer to be around those who are equally straightforward.

The age groups associated with this chakra are adolescence and the early teens. There is no particular sign of the zodiac that relates to this chakra—perhaps the crown chakra owes something to the whole zodiac, while those above it take something from the universe as a whole.

An Exaggerated Crown Chakra

These subjects may be unpleasant themselves, or they may be fine but suffer at the hands of those who are unpleasant, in the forms shown by either the exaggerated or deficient crown chakra.

Judgmental and moralistic, these people may have no problem imposing their starchy attitudes on others. They may consider themselves better than those around them. Some even use religion and spirituality to make others feel inadequate. Others take themselves very seriously, and may be religious bores that have no ordinary interests and no other topics of conversation. They are too wrapped up in the world of spirit to be able to function in the real world.

A Deficient Crown Chakra

Sometimes there is a problem in the relationship with the father, which makes early life very difficult, and this leaves a psychological mark. Sometimes there are family members who spot the fact that these folk are generous and spiritual, and take full advantage of their good natures. They must take care not to allow family members and others to drain them. Some of these people are too neurotic to enjoy life—they fear life and they fear death. If they live in difficult situations, they don't have the courage or strength to change their fate or to move away from it. They have no faith in the universe or even in their own futures, and can't progress.

These subjects may value money and goods more than people, beauty, or worthwhile activities, so they may become very rich, but lack soul or compassion. When some kind of severe loss comes along, these people may suddenly realize that there is more to life than moneymaking and start to take the first steps on the pathway to spiritual understanding.

Sometimes there is a desire to control or dominate others, or the person is obsessed with something and lacks balance. He might be too involved in the spiritual realm and lack practicality or common sense.

Body and Health

The crown chakra rules the brain, especially the right side of it, and it is also associated with the central nervous system. The following is a list of ailments associated with the crown chakra:

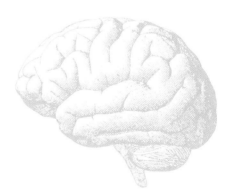

- Skin cancer
- Multiple sclerosis
- Schizophrenia
- Parkinson's disease
- Epilepsy
- Alzheimer's disease
- Bipolar disorder
- Depression
- Diseases of the eyes
- Varicose veins
- Eczema
- Rashes
- Warts
- Moles
- Bacterial infections

Correspondences

The corresponding ideas listed below are linked to the crown chakra. Some of these items come into their own when we apply complementary therapies or energy healing.

Vedic name:	Sahasrara
Other name:	Violet chakra
Number:	The seventh chakra
Color:	Violet, purple; in some traditions, white or gold
Gender:	Yin and Yang, thus masculine and feminine
Animal:	Angels
Lotus petals:	Purple lily or many petals
Shape:	Lotus, lily
Element:	Light
Planet:	Saturn
Zodiac signs:	Capricorn and Aquarius
Facial Area:	Head
Mantra:	Nnn
Music:	Silence

❉ ❉ ❉

3

THE MINOR CHAKRAS

The theory is that there are 78,000 chakras in the human body, but not everybody agrees on the number or where they are situated. You can find the chakras in your own body by keeping an eye on any aches and pains you may have or any areas that draw your attention. Many chakras mirror each other and are sited on both sides of the body, so if you notice two areas becoming itchy or irritated, it could be your mirrored chakras that are asking for healing. You may find out more about minor chakras through the internet or by talking to healers and psychics as well as your reflection on your own experience allied to common sense. It would be a good idea to take a photograph of yourself and mark in the extra chakras as you discover them.

Chakras Above the Body

The Eighth Chakra—Money and Death

The eighth chakra is located above the head. Some traditions say it sits immediately above the head, while others say it is sited several inches above the head. Some see this as a gold orb; others see it as a white glow or even a white flower.

Oddly enough, those who have spent a lifetime studying the chakras find people who are ruled by this chakra to be extremely money minded! So, if someone is ruled by the need to make or keep money, or to use it as a form of power over others, that person definitely needs healing to be directed to the eighth chakra. Those who are always broke could probably also benefit from healing to this chakra. As this is the chakra of big money, and also of old age and the end of life, there is a touch of Saturn and Capricorn about this one.

This chakra is said to be particularly important at the point of death, as some believe that the soul leaves the body from the crown of the head. This means the eighth chakra is the link between the mundane world and the next life, and that it carries some karma with it. However, this is not universally believed, as many psychics and those who work in hospitals and hospices have witnessed souls leaving bodies through the naval, as though attached to a new umbilical cord.

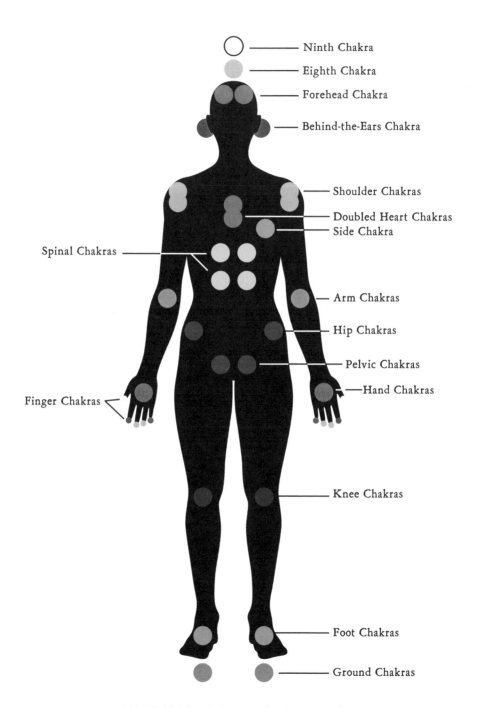

- Ninth Chakra
- Eighth Chakra
- Forehead Chakra
- Behind-the-Ears Chakra
- Shoulder Chakras
- Doubled Heart Chakras
- Side Chakra
- Spinal Chakras
- Arm Chakras
- Hip Chakras
- Pelvic Chakras
- Hand Chakras
- Finger Chakras
- Knee Chakras
- Foot Chakras
- Ground Chakras

DIAGRAM OF THE MINOR CHAKRAS

◯ The Ninth Chakra—Causes and Soapboxes

This chakra, which sits above the eight and is translucent white, is about saving the planet, caring for animals and plants, and helping others. It is a great chakra to invoke if you want to embark on anything of a humanitarian or idealistic nature. It seems to link astrologically to the planet Uranus and the sign of Aquarius.

> ### The Higher Chakras
>
> ••••◆◆◆◆◆••••
>
> Hindu tradition suggests that the upper chakras have a variety of spiritual purposes, but it may be hard for mere mortals to discover just what these are.

Chakras on the Body

● Forehead Chakras

Some people believe that there are two chakras on the forehead, which makes some sense, but others believe there is a vertical row of chakras on the forehead that runs from just above the brow chakra to the hairline. I'm not convinced about this one. Either way, the forehead chakras talk about intuition, relating with others, understanding the universe, and dealing with past and future lives.

● Behind-the-Ears Chakras

People or situations from a past life may hover around, causing the person to behave in a way that isn't appropriate. These people could even be controlled by discarnate entities and should have a clearance to get rid of these malign influences.

● Shoulder Chakras

I do have faith in shoulder chakras, because I am aware of them in my own body, and they seem to kick in when I do anything psychic. They run through the shoulders, from front to back. Some people say these are just above the armpits, but that is not my experience. Mine seem to be higher than this.

Side Chakra

Below the left armpit, there is a chakra that is involved with self-empowerment and the ability to stand up for oneself. If this chakra is too open, others will be able to take advantage of the person, while if it is blocked, he will be irritated and angry. There may be problems with the immune system.

Spinal Chakras

There are two chakras on each side of the spine that are said to link to higher learning. These sit just below the shoulder blades, so if you need to study something, focus on these points for a moment so that they will open up.

Doubled Heart Chakra

The lower heart chakra rules romantic love and the love of family, friends, children, and pets. When out of kilter, it can cause obsessive love, along with the sacral chakra, which is involved in sexual obsession. The upper heart chakra is more spiritual, so it is concerned with the love of angels, deities, spiritual guides, and the universe.

Arm Chakras

These chakras go through the elbows from the front to the back. They are associated with the flow of healing energy down the arms to the hands so they become active when someone is giving healing.

Hand Chakras

Every healer and many other psychics are aware that each hand has a chakra that runs through from the back to the hand to the palm.

Finger Chakras

Each fingertip has its own chakra. To see the effect of these, take a pendulum or use a pendant on a chain and hold this over your fingers one at a time. The pendulum will revolve in a different direction over each finger. If you don't get any reaction, try working on someone else's hands, because the interaction between you might make it work more successfully than doing it on yourself. In practical terms, these chakras give help when you are healing or helping others.

Hip Chakras

These chakras sit on the sides of the body, going through from the front to the back. Give them a rub when you need to feel protected and confident.

Pelvic Chakras

Chakras on either side of the pelvic area can give you confidence, so focus your mind on them for a moment when you need to feel more in control of your life.

Knee Chakras

These chakras are said to go through the knees from one side to the other, but I have discovered that they actually work through the leg from the front of the knee to the back. They are said to open when one is praying or asking the angels for help.

Foot Chakras

Foot chakras go through the insteps and out through the soles of the feet, although some traditions say they are under the heels. These chakras are activated whenever you do a grounding meditation. If you're feeling extremely nervous or tense, try sending light down through your body and through the soles of your feet to the ground below, as it will help you calm down. Standing on sand or grass can also help you to ground yourself.

Chakras Below the Body

Ground Chakras

There is a theory that the ground beneath the feet has a chakra-type effect. If this chakra is blocked, it can engender feelings of helplessness and an inability to cope with the practicalities of daily life. This area is sensitive to geopathic stressors, such as power line towers, polluted areas, too much water running at the back of the home or workplace, or something toxic in the environment.

One way to help balance this chakra area is to sit with some brown stones—such as tiger's eye, agate, or flint—near the feet and meditate on the need for calmness, mental balance, and a clear mind.

✳ ✳ ✳

4

IDENTIFYING WEAK CHAKRAS

At any one time in our lives, some chakras will be strong while one or two may be weak or misaligned, and the causes can by physical, emotional, or spiritual. For instance, if you go through a phase of winter colds and chest infections, it is obvious that the throat and heart chakras need healing. A twisted ankle will benefit from healing to the foot chakras and also to the base chakra, because that chakra also influences the legs and feet. Headaches call for treatment to the crown and brow chakras, but also the throat chakra due to its connection to the jaw and the upper spine, where tension headaches can arise.

A person may have one or more of the main chakras that aren't working properly, and if the person is very ill or suffering some deep trauma, the aura and all the chakras will be temporarily weakened. The following is designed to help you identify those chakras that might be weak, blocked, or malfunctioning. The ideas below will help you do this.

- Look through the checklist information below for areas in which you're having issues or want to improve.
- Use a pendulum to find the problems; I will go into this later in this chapter.
- Work through the brief quiz at the end of this chapter.
- Consult an energy healer who has the ability to see or feel the chakras and to work out which of yours isn't/aren't fully functioning.

The Chakra Checklist

Base Chakra

- Concern for our basic needs, such as a home, job, transportation to and from work, money and possessions. Survival instinct, safety.
- Love of music and rhythm especially rock music and drumming.
- Love of nature and sexuality.
- Reproductive organs, waste elimination, and cell reproduction.

Sacral Chakra

- Need for connection, happiness, and openness with others.
- Healthy emotions, a good sex life, and happiness in personal relationships.
- Good relationships at work with bosses, coworkers, and colleagues.
- Creativity.
- Reproductive organs, adrenaline, kidneys, and digestive system.

Solar Plexus Chakra

- Well-directed willpower, leadership, managerial skills, and the ability to succeed in one's career.
- The mind, intelligence, and ability to study and teach.
- A happy family and a well-run home.
- Liver, spleen, pancreas, and intestines.

Heart Chakra

- Compassion and empathy for others, unconditional love, the emotions.
- Generosity and good relationships.
- Sufficient income and funds to live in comfort.
- Immune system, circulation, and heart.

Throat Chakra

- Communications ability, common sense, intelligence, and logic.
- The ability to listen to others and to empathize.
- The truth, creativity, and judging the shape and size of things around us.
- Vocal chords, larynx, thyroid system, hearing, and lymphatic system.

Brow Chakra

- Clear thinking, good mind, and imagination.
- Clairvoyance, spirituality, ESP, inner wisdom, intuition, and psychism.
- Being honest, reliable, compassionate, decent, and capable.
- Nervous system and skull.

Crown Chakra

- Idealism, humanitarianism, generosity, helpfulness, and being able to link with spirit.
- Valuing spiritual rather than material aspirations, along with psychic gifts.
- Linking with the universe, deities, and the higher consciousness.
- Brain, spirituality, and spiritual defense systems.

Minor Chakras

The most important of these is probably the eighth chakra, which is just above the head, and this is said to be the gateway between this world and the next. Negatively, it may manifest in too much emphasis on making and keeping money, while lack of equilibrium and a lack of common sense might also rule here.

Astrology and Elements

If you are into astrology or if you like working the four elements of fire, earth, air, and water, here are some basic traits that you might like to consider. If you have a particular element strongly marked on your chart, you will soon start to get a feel for the chakras connected to it. There are twelve signs of the zodiac but only seven chakras, two of which are linked to one sign and five of which are assigned to two signs, so as you will see it makes an awkward fit. The table on page 22 will help you see these links.

The Fire Group (Masculine)

ARIES, LEO, SAGITTARIUS If you belong to a fire sign, you will think and act quickly and you will be quick to take up opportunities when they come along. You have powerful leadership qualities. You can be selfish at times, simply because you don't always stop and look at the way your actions impinge on those around you. However, your heart is in the right place and you are idealistic, spontaneous, loving, and generous. You are less confident than you appear to be, and you can become depressed when too much goes wrong. There are two signs linked to the base chakra but only one of them is a fire sign. There is one sign linked to the solar plexus chakra and two to the crown chakra, one of which is a fire sign. The fire signs that are linked to the chakras are as follows:

| Chakra Links | Base (Aries) | Solar plexus (Leo) | Brow (Sagittarius) |

The Earth Group (Feminine)

TAURUS, VIRGO, CAPRICORN You are practical, sensible, and hardworking, and you can be relied on to do what is asked of you. You do not rush at things, because you prefer to work at your own pace. Security is important to you, both in the financial sense and in your personal relationships. You are shrewd in business and perhaps a little too materialistic, but at least you are prepared to provide for yourself and your family. There are two signs linked to the heart chakra but only one of them is an earth sign; the same goes for the throat and the crown chakras. The earth signs that are linked to the chakras are as follows:

Chakra Links	Heart (Taurus)	Throat (Virgo)	Crown (Capricorn)

The Air Group (Masculine)

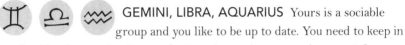 **GEMINI, LIBRA, AQUARIUS** Yours is a sociable group and you like to be up to date. You need to keep in touch with others and to know what is going on in your environment. In business, you prefer to meet people face to face and to communicate in a clear and open manner. You are not particularly clever with money, but you work hard and generally stay out of debt. Tension and worry get you down. Being a little detached, you can't cope with an emotionally dependent partner. There are two signs linked to the heart chakra but only one of them is an air sign. There are two signs linked to the throat chakra but only one of them is an air sign, while Aquarius doesn't appear anywhere. The air signs that are linked to the chakras are as follows:

Chakra Links	Heart (Libra)	Throat (Gemini)	Crown (Aquarius)

The Water Group (Feminine)

CANCER, SCORPIO, PISCES You may appear slow on the uptake because you need time to think about things before committing yourself, but your intuition is strong and you can rely on it to guide you. Your shrewdness and intuition can make you a successful businessperson. Because your emotions and feelings run deep, you can be badly hurt. You love deeply and rarely let your friends or loved ones down. There are two signs linked to the base chakra but only one is a water sign. There is one sign linked to the sacral chakra and that is a water sign, but two signs are linked to the brow chakra, one of which is a water sign. The water signs that are linked to the chakras are as follows:

Chakra Links	Base (Scorpio)	Sacral (Cancer)	Brow (Pisces)

Finding Chakra Problems with a Pendulum

A pendulum can be as simple as a heavy needle threaded onto a length of cotton string, or you can use a necklace made of fine chain that has a pendant on it. Both of these solutions are all right if you don't have anything else on hand, but if you wish to carry out spiritual work on a regular basis, it is always worth buying the right equipment for the purpose.

There are plenty of pendulums available in shops or on websites that

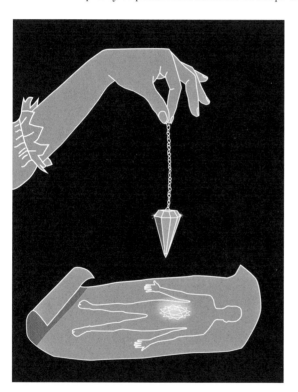

specialize in spiritual goods—or you can find them at mind, body, and spirit festivals. Fortunately, they are inexpensive. You can choose a pendulum with a crystal, a piece of shaped glass, a specially carved piece of wood, or a simple metal weight. I find wood too lightweight, so I prefer to work with glass or a crystal, but it is a matter of personal preference. I suggest that you put the pendulum in a pretty bag or pouch to keep it safe and clean when

you aren't using it, store it out of sight of children and pets, and use it only for spiritual work.

Once you have your pendulum, you need to clean the residue that has accumulated on it by being handled by other people or by lying around in a dusty shop or warehouse. Wash the pendulum thoroughly in bottled spring water or in rainwater; dry it carefully with paper towels; then leave it outside where it can benefit from being in the open air for a while. Now hold your pendulum in your hands and imagine white light coming down from the universe onto the pendulum. Ask your angels, deity, or spiritual guides to bless the pendulum and to make it work for the benefit of those who need help.

It is a good idea to take the time to "attune" your pendulum before you use it the first time, and you do this by holding the pendulum by the chain or thread and mentally asking it to show you how it would react when it wants to give you a positive, "yes" answer. It may make a circular movement in a clockwise or a counterclockwise direction or it may move from side to side or oscillate forward and back. Then ask the pendulum to give you a "no" answer and see what happens. Now you will know when you are getting a positive reading to anything that you ask of it, but there are some subtle differences that you need to take on board when you go hunting for chakras.

Marking Troubled Chakras

Normally, copying or photocopying something from a book is a breach of copyright, but for this particular task, I give you my permission to make plenty of photocopies of the man and woman sketches on the following pages.

Take a photocopy of a sketch, put the person's name on it and the date. As you find each chakra, mark it on a photocopy so that you have a record of where each one is. If you feel that a chakra is performing well, mark it in green or blue, but if you sense that a chakra is blocked or troubled, mark it in red.

Using a Pendulum

Ask a friend to lie down somewhere comfortable, and mentally ask your pendulum to show you where each chakra is located. Start by holding the pendulum over one of your friend's feet at a distance of about six inches, and see if the pendulum reacts. The pendulum may circle round in one direction for one foot and the other for the other foot, or it may move from side to side for one foot and up and done for the other. Now move up to your friend's knees and see whether you can pick up anything there.

Now work your way up the body, picking up one chakra after another. When it comes to the "mirrored" chakras—by which I mean one on each side of the body, as in the shoulders or hips—you will find the pendulum reversing, or going in a different direction for each. When you work your way up the main chakras that line up along the spine, the pendulum should reverse its motion from one to the next.

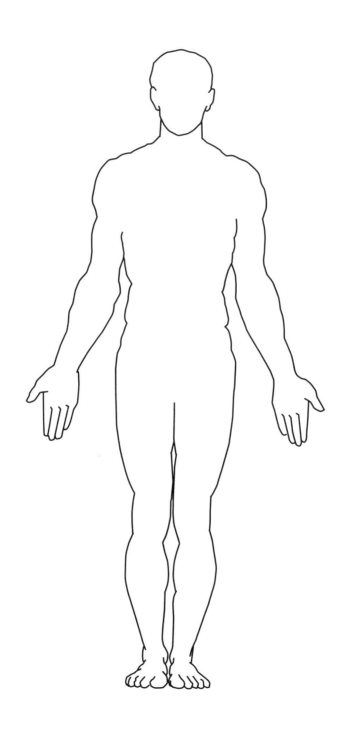

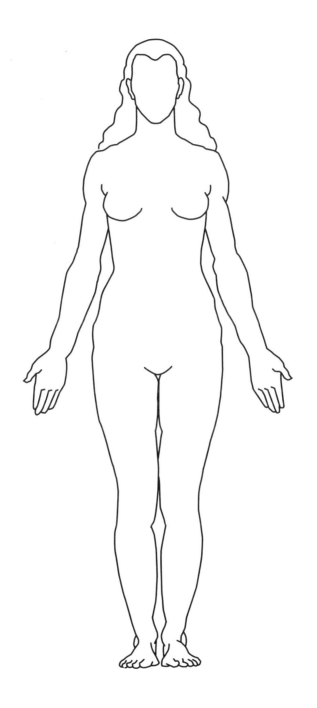

On the hands, each palm will show a chakra, as will each fingertip, and each will move in a different way to the other. Some might spin or sway from side to side or forward and back.

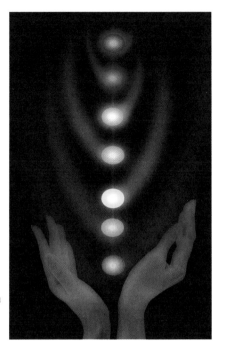

A Malfunctioning Chakra

It's easy to discover which chakra needs healing, since the pendulum will struggle to move when it reaches it. This is particularly obvious when it comes to the seven main chakras because the illustrations in this book show you where they are situated, so if you reach a spot where there should definitely be a chakra and the pendulum struggles to move, you know you have found the problem.

An Exaggerated Chakra

If one chakra reacts much more than the others do, it is probably overdoing things, possibly because it is compensating for a nearby chakra that isn't working properly.

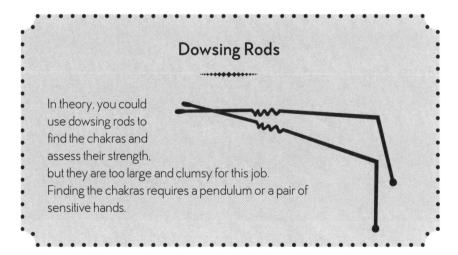

Dowsing Rods

In theory, you could use dowsing rods to find the chakras and assess their strength, but they are too large and clumsy for this job. Finding the chakras requires a pendulum or a pair of sensitive hands.

A PERSONAL NOTE

I have tried out pendulum dowsing on my husband, Peter. Interestingly, I discovered that, despite the fact that ancient wisdom suggested the chakras that go through the knees do so from side to side, I discovered that his chakras definitely went through the knees from front to back. I also found two chakras in each shoulder area, with one at the shoulder joint and another just above the armpit. This solved the argument of exactly where the shoulder chakras are situated, as there seem to be two in each shoulder.

Feeling Energy

Some people can feel energy through their hands—these sensitive people could even dowse a desert for water with nothing more than their bare hands. A way of seeing whether you can feel energy is to put your hands together as though you were praying, then draw them apart to a distance of about eighteen inches, then bring your hands slowly together, stopping when you feel a sense of pressure. It might feel as though you  were bouncing your hands on an invisible balloon. The pressure that you feel is the aura coming from both of your hands and meeting in the gap between them. If you can feel this kind of pressure, you could try passing your hands over your friend's body at a distance of about six inches and see what you can pick up. A sense of pressure coming from a chakra shows that it is working, but if the power seems too great in comparison with the other chakras, it might be overworking, maybe in compensation for some other chakra that isn't working properly.

A Chakra Quiz

The simple quiz below comprises a few questions that might also help you identify any weak chakras. Tick the relevant boxes, and you will see the chakras listed in the final column.

To make life easy, here are the seven main chakras by number, including the eighth chakra that is above the subject's head.

1. Base
2. Sacral
3. Solar Plexus
4. Heart

5. Throat
6. Brow
7. Crown
8. Upper

Topic	Yes	Sometimes	Chakra/s
I worry about keeping a roof over my head and feeding my family.			1
I have enough for my needs but could do with more.			1, 2
I would enjoy my work more if I was with bosses and colleagues I like.			2, 3, 4
I want to be in a partnership, and I miss it when there is nobody with whom to make love.			2, 4
I appreciate beauty for its own sake more than what things cost, but there isn't much beauty in my surroundings.			4, 6
I love my friends and family and I want them to love me back.			4
I ask everyone's opinion when I have a decision to make.			3, 5
I want to do more creative, pictorial, or artistic work.			3, 6

I pray or ask my spiritual guides for help when I have a decision to make, but I am not sure they hear me.			5, 7
I would love to heal and help others but don't have the confidence to do so.			4, 7
I hate being pushed around and want to know how to stop that happening.			3, 5
I wish I could do more to help the planet and the environment.			1, 6, 7
I feel that I am drifting through life with no connection to God or the universe.			7, 8
I would like it if my family actually listened to me and understood my point of view.			5
I would love to travel and learn more about the world, but I can't at the moment.			3, 5
I would feel more successful if I had more money.			1, 2, 8
I wish I understood the universe's purpose.			7, 8
I wish I could sense trouble before it comes.			6
I love to help others but I get used, and I wish I could get help from others when I am in need of it.			3, 4, 5
I am in the depths of despair and need help.			All the chakras

❋ ❋ ❋

PART II
CHAKRA
HEALING

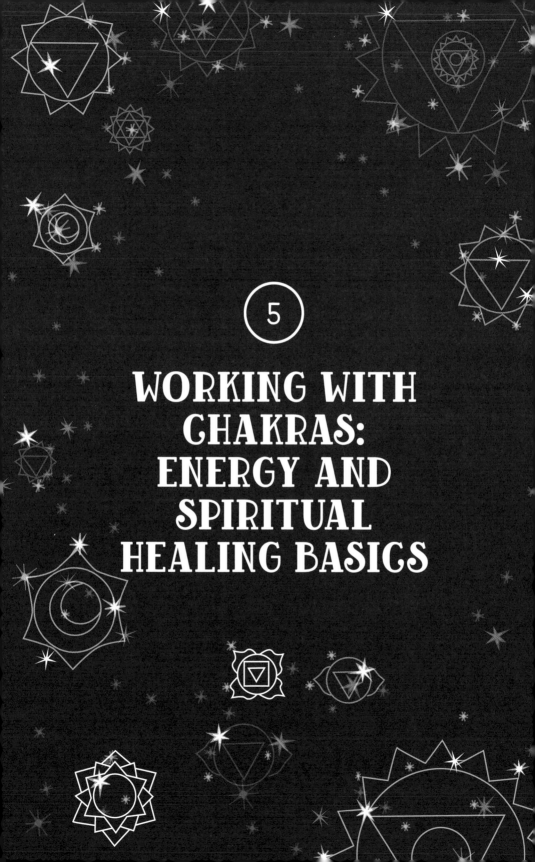

5

WORKING WITH CHAKRAS: ENERGY AND SPIRITUAL HEALING BASICS

The term *energy healing* has come into use in recent years, and it is so descriptive that I can't think of a better one. A number of methods come under its umbrella, but when the hype is stripped away, it comes down to the ability to harness healing energy and feed it to the person who needs it. Sometimes the healing is directed specifically at the chakras; in other cases, it is simply transmitted to the recipient, whereupon the chakras may pick it up and make use of it.

Unless the healer happens to be a doctor, it's not a good idea to attempt to give a specific diagnosis, but any half-decent psychic can sense the *area* of the body that is unwell, and hopefully the precise chakras that would benefit from healing.

Energy healing is noninvasive; it doesn't put any product onto or into the body, and the subject stays fully clothed. One or two healers can work on a person who is seated or perhaps stretched out on a therapy couch. They use their connection to "spirit" to channel the energy through themselves and out through their hands, directing the energy into the client's chakras. A good method is to bring down white light—flecked with pale blue for health, white light flecked with pale green for emotional ones, or flecked with pale lavender for spiritual ones—and pour this into the chakras.

When healing someone at a distance, the healer can make a sketch of the client or use a photo. He might hold a pendulum an inch or two above the image, until drawn to a particular part of the body, and then send a blast of healing light to the distant client, focusing in particular on the area of weakness.

There is also what I call "batch healing," whereby a healer sends out healing to a number of people whose names are on a list. In this case, it doesn't matter what the clients are suffering from, only that they are on the receiving end of a blast of healing energy. The best way to do this is to ask the clients to focus on the healer on a particular day and at a prearranged time, and then the healer sends out the healing. My feeling is that it won't work if the healer just sends out healing without the clients being tuned in, but that is just my opinion.

How Energy and Spiritual Healing Works

Because energy healing is noninvasive, it can't do any harm. The only downside is that the client might expect an instant miracle cure. While this can happen on occasion, for the most part it takes several sessions for the healing to work. Some clients won't benefit from the healing because they have an unexpressed psychological need to stay sick.

Spiritual healing is *not* faith healing, and the healer doesn't need to belong to a church or believe in a special god or deity; indeed, the only *real* requirement is that the client wants to get well. The idea behind this form of healing is that the healer taps into a source of energy, and sends it out through his or her hands to the client.

The source that the healer taps into might be a deity, an angel, an archangel (especially Raphael), a spiritual guide, an ancestor in spirit, the universe, nature, an ascended master, or the healer's own higher consciousness. In the simplest terms, energy is drawn into the healer's body, often by visualizing white light (sometimes with flecks of other colors), which is drawn into the healer, probably via his crown chakra.

The client is normally seated on a straight chair or stool, which enables the healer to walk around the client and pour healing in from different directions. This may not be directed at the chakras as such, but it will reach them anyway.

The healer may gently hold the client's head and shoulders in his hands, but many healers prefer to hold their hands a short distance away from the client, and this is especially the case as the healer works his way down the client's body. The healer will work on the client's back and then come around to the front so that he can work on the legs and feet. If the healer feels drawn to the part of the body that needs healing, he may pay extra attention to this.

The client may feel warmth, tingling, or some other sensation as the healing takes place, or may feel nothing at all, but it will still work as it feeds into the chakras and kick-starts the body's own regenerative power.

Spirituality

It is sometimes hard for people to know their true spiritual path, but after someone gives healing to the brow and crown chakras, the spiritual world will find ways of showing the person what their path should be. This can come in very strange ways, perhaps by seeing a particular image turning up in shop windows, or as advertisements on passing vehicles or even as shapes in a cloud. The person may hear music that reminds him of something, or there may be significant dreams. A meditation session after a healing session will open his mind and heart to possibilities that he might not otherwise have considered.

Opening the Chakras

If you wish to give energy healing or spiritual
healing, do any psychic work, or carry out a deep
meditation, you will need to open the chakras.
Once you have finished your work, you will need
to close them again in order to avoid feeling
spacey or having bad dreams or uncomfortable
feelings over the next day or two.

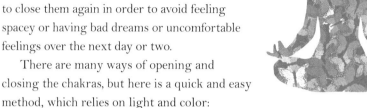

There are many ways of opening and
closing the chakras, but here is a quick and easy
method, which relies on light and color:

- Start by imagining white light coming down from the universe and
  see it reaching your *crown chakra*, which is on the top of your head.
  As it arrives, visualize a purple flower opening there and allowing the
  light to enter your body.

- Allow the white light to fill the crown of your head and to reach your
  forehead, where a large blue eye opens. This is your *brow chakra.*

- Now let the light reach your *throat chakra*, where a turquoise blue light
  comes on. This light runs from the front to the back of your body.

- Let the light come down to your chest area where your *heart chakra*
  lies, and let a green light come on and shine from the front to the
  back of your body. Also, let it fill your arms and hands.

- Now do the same for your *solar plexus chakra*, which is just above your
  naval, and let a yellow light come on.

- Take the light down to your *sacral chakra*, which is in the middle of
  your abdomen; this light is colored orange.

- Take the light down to the base of your body, which is where the *base
  chakra* is, and let a red light come on.

- Let the light fill your legs and feet, and run the light down into the
  earth below.

Closing the Chakras

Start by bringing the light up from the earth into your feet and legs and turn it off, then turn off the white lights and all the colored lights while you reverse the procedure for opening the chakras. Ensure that you close the brow chakra eye and the flower at the crown of your head. Send the light back up to the universe, and mentally ask that it be sent to give healing to those who need it.

If you feel lightheaded after doing any kind of spiritual work, take your shoes off and walk around on grass, sand, or earth. If that isn't practical, imagine that you are wrapping yourself in a purple blanket, as this will afford you some spiritual protection while the spacey feeling eases off.

When You Have Finished Healing

I recently read a very old book that said that after a healing session, the healer should shake his hands to rid himself of the energies that he might have picked up from his client. I dislike this idea as someone may unwittingly walk through the area where the "psychic dirt" has been tossed. It is far better for the healer simply to wash his hands, but if he is working in a place without washing facilities nearby, he should provide himself with a dish with some salt in it, and when he's finished his healing sessions, he  should brush or shake his hands over the salt. Salt is a very cleansing material, so it will absorb the "psychic dirt" and neutralize it.

Healing as a Profession

Only touch those people who know you well and who aren't likely to take the opportunity to sue you for some kind of imaginary "inappropriate" behavior. If you take up healing in a serious manner, it is better to work in a group environment, such as a spiritualist church, a healing center, or a psychic fair. You should also ensure that the organization is insured against accidents and accusations. If you work alone, *always* have someone in the room with you while the healing takes place. This applies when you are working on a person of your own sex as well as working on someone of the opposite sex.

While we're on the subject, if you wish to become a professional healer or consultant in tarot, astrology, a therapy, or something similar, you should take out public liability, professional indemnity, and medical malpractice insurance. Public liability insurance covers you in case of accidents and damage to someone's goods or person, while personal indemnity insurance and medical malpractice insurance cover you for accusations of professional negligence, inappropriate behavior, and much else.

If you don't know where to start, go to my website www.mbsprofessionals. com for information and assistance.

Qualifications

If you have learned your skill and wish to become professional, you must join a recognized organization and take the necessary qualifications. You can work without qualifications in many countries, as long as you don't charge a fee, but you should still take training and become qualified.

Lessons

There are groups of people who are into the same things as you, and organizations that give training, either in person or online. If you can't get to meetings or classes, try the internet, because you will find lessons and healing sessions of many kinds on YouTube and elsewhere.

Ego

You are a channel that allows the healing power to pass through in order to do its work. It isn't you who does the healing but a source such as God, some other deity, angels, ascended masters, or the universe. Anything to which you feel attuned will work, as long as you let the source flow through you and you don't allow your ego to get in the way.

Not Everyone Wants to Get Well

Astonishing as it may seem, there are people who have a vested interest in hanging on to their ailments, which may be due to psychological reasons or something crafty and manipulative. Whatever the reason, if someone doesn't want healing, don't insist they have it, and if someone receives healing but refuses to be healed . . . well, I can only suggest that you write it off to experience.

Do No Harm

Work for the benefit of others and *always* work in the blessed side of life. *Never* set out to do harm to anyone, even if you can't stand them. It's worth bearing in mind that bad actions have a way of coming back on the person who sends them. Frankly, I wouldn't wish to give healing to someone I loathed, so if I were asked, I would politely refuse and let another healer take over.

Set Your Intention

Before you begin any healing session, work out what you want to achieve and how you want to go about it. This is called "setting your intention." Always work for the benefit of the person to whom you are giving healing.

6

REIKI HEALING FOR FOR CHAKRAS

Reiki is similar to spiritual healing, but it uses specific hand positions that reach the chakras while the healing occurs. Reiki healers carry images of certain symbols in mind while giving the healing. The Reiki healer doesn't tap into a spiritual guide, but rather into the "Reiki lineage," which is a spiritual connection with the people who created the Reiki system and who endorsed and extended its use around the world.

Reiki is more than just a healing system—it is a road to spiritual awareness that helps the adherent to live a happy life. It includes regular spiritual empowerments, the twenty-one-day palm-healing cleanse, meditations, breathing exercises, visualizations, mantras, mystical symbols, and five Reiki precepts, all of which make Reiki unique as a healing and spiritual system. It is a massive subject that I will go into only in a superficial way here.

The Reiki healer starts by working on himself for several months before he begins giving healing to clients. Before his client comes for the consultation, he meditates to raise his own energies and life force so that he is ready to give the healing. The healer shouldn't wear any jewelry, and if the client is wearing any, he or she should take it off. Now the client lies down on a therapy couch while the healer washes his hands and says a silent prayer that asks for healing to be given to his client.

The healer gently runs his hands over his client's aura from a distance of about eight inches, smoothing out the aura while tuning in to the client. He places his hands on the client's head, covering the forehead and eyes, keeping the hands in place for a few moments in order to relieve the client of a host of chronic ailments.

The healer now moves to the side of the client's head.

He then places his hands on the back of the client's head.

Then he moves to various other parts of the body in a special sequence while pouring in the Reiki healing through his hands. The practitioner might feel a variety of sensations, such as being drawn to a problem area of the body, becoming aware of pain and inflammation, and so on.

REIKI MASTERS

An ascended master is someone who lived on earth and had great spiritual healing ability when he or she was alive, and this power has now become available to those who wish to tap into it. For Christians, this might be Jesus Christ or a particular saint, while for those who are Reiki practitioners, the link is with Mikao Usui, who was the original founder of the Reiki system.

The point is that the healer is a *channel* or *conduit* for the healing energy. He doesn't have any power of his own, just the ability to channel energy to his client. I think of this in terms of electricity, because an electric wire can't do anything until it is connected to a source of electricity at one end and then it delivers electricity to the relevant piece of equipment or machinery at the other end.

Reiki and the Chakras

Here is a brief reminder of the problems related to each of the seven main chakras, from a Reiki healer's point of view:

The Base Chakra

This is the site of Kundalini, so it needs to be in good order for all the other chakras to work properly. It relates to problems with the bones or the bowels, along with aggression and mental problems of various kinds. It is concerned with fear and the basic needs for survival.

The Sacral Chakra

This chakra rules bladder and kidney problems, lymphatic problems, and problems related to sex and reproduction. It relates to sexual love and the need for companionship, along with phobias, obsessive-compulsive disorders, and fussiness.

The Solar Plexus Chakra

This chakra rules the gallbladder, liver, pancreas, and spleen, so it relates to diabetes and digestive disorders. It is the center of personal power and strength, and it can relate to guilt or a desire to escape a pressured situation. Greed and selfishness are possible, but lack of self-worth, insecurity, fear of being disliked, and fear of failure are also possible.

The Heart Chakra

The heart, the circulation, and the lungs are ruled here, but there is also a lot of emotional baggage linked to this chakra: selfishness and manipulation of others on one hand, but also confidence and self-acceptance.

The Throat Chakra

Problems with the throat chakra could affect growth and development, but also the throat, neck, speech, and hearing. The person may find it difficult to express his feelings and may find it hard to speak up on his own behalf, but on the other hand, he may be arrogant and apt to order others around.

The Brow Chakra

A weak brow chakra could lead to problems with the eyes and even the upper teeth, but it can also make for a disorganized person who can't finish anything that he starts. This person finds it hard to study and has little intuition or spirituality.

The Crown Chakra

This chakra may relate to the brain. It also connects with spirituality and karma. If the chakra malfunctions, the person may have no interest in spiritual matters, a strange attitude, or be drawn to the more extreme forms of belief.

Chakra Healing Through Reiki

The Reiki healer holds his hands about eight to ten inches above the above chakras in a special pattern, while beaming down Reiki visualizations and healing power.

- He treats the base chakra and the brow chakra at the same time.
- He treats the sacral chakra and the throat chakra at the same time.
- He treats the solar plexus chakra and the heart chakra at the same time.

A system that makes much more sense to me is to ask the client to stand sideways on, while the practitioner places his hands some inches away from the body, dealing with both the front and back of any chakra that seems to be giving a problem.

Tip

I have always heard that it is *not* a good idea for a healer to place his hands on the crown of a client's head, and this seems to be borne out by what I have discovered in my research of Reiki.

Minor Chakras

The minor chakras link to the blessings and detractions of some of the seven main chakras, so if there are problems with the main ones, the Reiki healer might decide to work on these minor ones instead of the client's main body. This is how the connections work:

- The palm chakras link to the sacral, solar plexus, and heart chakras.
- The elbow chakras link to the sacral and solar plexus chakras.
- The shoulder chakras link to the solar plexus and throat chakras.
- The foot chakras link to the base and solar plexus chakras.
- The knee chakras link to the throat and brow chakras.

❋ ❋ ❋

7

CRYSTAL HEALING FOR CHAKRAS

If you want to clear a blocked or misaligned chakra, you can choose crystals that link directly to that chakra. For instance, obsidian or red jasper can clear the base chakra, or lapis lazuli can clear the throat chakra. If you want to enliven one of the upper chakras, such as the heart, throat, brow, or crown chakra, you could use a "warming" crystal, such as garnet or carnelian, and if you want to calm down an overworked or overheated lower chakra, such as the base, sacral or solar plexus, you could use something like blue lace agate, jade, or clear quartz. Whatever you choose to do, crystal healing can't do any harm.

Preparing Crystals for Chakra Healing

Before using any crystals, special stones, or metals, you need to clear any dust and dirt from them, and then rid them of any negative energy they have picked up by being touched by people in the past. Wash your crystals in rainwater or bottled spring water. Don't use mineral water as the salts in it might damage the crystals. Once your crystals are clean, leave them outside in a safe place for twenty-four hours to let them gather the power of the sun and the moon into themselves. This will work if it's cloudy, but it will work even better if the sky is clear. Once you have cleansed your crystals, take them in your hands

and imagine white light coming down from the universe. Ask for the crystals to be blessed and for them to help you and others whenever they are used.

When you aren't using your crystals, keep them in a pretty box where they won't get jumbled together and damaged, and keep them away from children and pets. From time to time, reenergize your crystals by wafting them in the smoke of an incense stick and asking the universe to bless them and make them helpful to you and to others.

Tip

Some stones will dissolve in liquid, so clean these by giving them a rubdown with a paper towel. Then light an incense stick and hold the stones in the smoke while asking the universe to bless them and give them the strength they need for the healing they will be asked to perform.

Crystal Healing Procedure

Ask the person you want to heal to lie down somewhere comfortable. This can even be on the floor, on top of a blanket or comforter. Now you have a choice because you can place the relevant crystals, stones, or metals *beside* the subject, lining up with the chakras, or you can hold an appropriate crystal *over* a chakra for a few minutes, holding it about six or eight inches over the person's body.

If you are giving healing to yourself, or if you are helping someone else but aren't in a suitable place for your recipient to lie down, you can do it this way: To heal yourself, hold a crystal in your hand and focus on sending the crystal energy to the relevant chakra. To heal someone else, ask the client to hold the crystal in his hand, while focusing on sending the energies to the relevant chakra.

Tip

If you don't have a crystal that would be just right for the job, use a clear crystal, as it will help in all circumstances.

If you feel that the person needs some extra grounding, place a black or brown crystal beside each foot.

Common Crystals for Common Problems

These inexpensive crystals are easy to find and can help many common problems:

Clear Quartz

This clear stone can take the place of any crystal and be used to clear any problem and to encourage the body to heal itself, whether from a physical problem or a mental, emotional, or spiritual one.

Rose Quartz

This rose-colored stone has a couple of really useful properties. First, it will help heal a broken heart or promote feelings of love. Second, it can bring comfort and consolation at times of stress and trauma.

Amber

This warm, golden stone is not a crystal at all, but a solidified piece of tree resin that could easily be a million years old, so it has seen just about everything! It has healing properties, especially for colds and common ailments that aren't life threatening but are irritating nevertheless. From ancient times, amber has been considered helpful during labor and childbirth, so put a little of it on the bedside table of any woman who is in the throes of childbirth.

Carnelian

This pinkie-orange stone calms down those who are feeling frustrated and irritable, helps with financial problems, and brings solace and happiness. It also helps the blood circulation.

Amethyst

This purple and white stone is linked to spirituality and
the higher consciousness, so it aids psychic perception. It is
also protective—keep it in a pocket if you are in troubling
situations. A piece of amethyst on your bedside table or under
your pillow will bring sweet dreams and a good night's sleep.

Blue Lace Agate

A piece of this lovely pale blue stone on or near your
computer or any machinery will help it to keep going and not
to crash. It is a calming stone that is also good for all-around
health, so a little piece of it in your pocket or purse will help
in stressful situations.

Sodalite

This isn't the prettiest of stones, as it can look like a dark
blue and white lump of rock, but it has healing properties
that can help lower blood pressure and clear a confused and
busy mind.

Tiger's Eye

This lovely brown-and-gold stone gives a boost of confidence
when it is needed, and it can bring feelings of security. It
is said to help with digestive problems and the nervous
conditions that cause them.

Red Jasper

This is a great stone to carry with you when you need a boost
of courage and confidence.

Obsidian and Snowflake Obsidian

Either of these stones is great for times when you need
protection or if you need something you use on a regular
basis to work as it should. Put a piece of this stone in your
vehicle or by your computer or machinery to keep it from
harmful influences. Keep a piece in your purse or pocket if you are likely to be
among people who are not on your side.

Clearing Sluggish Chakras

Once you have identified the chakras that need to be cleared or realigned or to work in a calm and comfortable manner, use any of the crystals that are relevant to each chakra from the suggestions below.

Base Chakra

- Black onyx
- Garnet
- Hematite
- Red jasper
- Mahogany jasper
- Pyrite
- Ruby
- Obsidian
- Flint
- Red aventurine
- Black tourmaline
- Bloodstone
- Metal—iron

Sacral Chakra

- Amber
- Aventurine
- Carnelian
- Citrine
- Tiger's eye
- Coral
- Jasper
- Moonstone
- Fire opal
- Topaz
- Peach selenite
- Orange calcite
- Sunstone
- Metal—silver

Solar Plexus Chakra

- Yellow amber
- Amethyst
- Calcite
- Citrine
- Sodalite
- Tiger's eye
- Topaz
- Yellow fluorite
- Yellow jasper
- Honey calcite
- Metal—gold

Heart Chakra

- Aventurine
- Emerald
- Jade
- Chrysocolla
- Agate
- Peridot
- Rose quartz
- Malachite
- Moonstone
- Pink tourmaline
- Green tourmaline
- Copper
- Green fluorite
- Mangano calcite
- Rhodonite
- Metal—copper

Throat Chakra

- Turquoise
- Aquamarine
- Lapis lazuli
- Blue lace agate
- Sodalite
- Amazonite
- Celestine
- Fluorite
- Sapphire
- Cinnabar
- Chrysoprase
- Chrysocolla
- Blue tourmaline
- Metal—mercury

Brow Chakra

- Clear quartz
- Lapis lazuli
- Amethyst
- Azurite
- Calcite
- Dark sapphire
- Fluorite
- Sodalite
- Tanzanite
- Metal—tin

Crown Chakra

- Diamond
- Zircon
- Amethyst
- Pearl
- Clear quartz
- Rose quartz
- Howlite
- Herkimer diamond
- Danburite
- White jade
- Metal—white gold or lead

✳ ✳ ✳

8

HEALING CHAKRAS WITH COLOR

Complementary therapies are ideal for some chronic ailments where conventional medicine can do little to help, and the same goes for some stress-related ailments. Other ailments that are well served by conventional medicine or even psychotherapy may be healed more quickly or eased by the use of complementary therapies or energy healing.

All complementary therapies work through the chakras, but they don't all work in the same way. For example, herbal or essential oil treatment that stimulates a body that is being slowed by rheumatism or muscle weakness will help to make the lower chakras spin properly and thus speed up healing. Anything that works in a calming manner, such as aromatherapy, reflexology, or Reiki, is helpful in the case of chest infections, inflammatory ailments, and headaches, as calm is particularly beneficial to the upper chakras.

If you are receiving conventional medical treatment, remember to tell your doctor about any complementary treatments that you are using, especially those that you ingest or that are absorbed into the body, such as homeopathy, herbal treatments, or aromatherapy.

Check Credentials

If you decide to consult a practitioner in *any* complementary or alternative therapy, check that they are fully qualified in their discipline, that they have a certificate displayed on their wall, and that they are fully insured with public liability, professional indemnity, and medical malpractice insurance.

Color Healing Basics

Let us start with the basics of color healing methods that are safe enough to use on others, or for you to ask others to use on you. As color is so heavily associated with the chakras—and with the aura—we will begin with main color ideas. The first is very simple because it is a matter of choosing to eat fruits and vegetables of the appropriate color for a day or so. Here are some ideas:

Fruits and Vegetables

Base chakra: Cherries, tomatoes, red plums, red peppers, strawberries, and raspberries

Sacral chakra: Oranges, tangerines, carrots, apricots, and orange peppers

Solar plexus chakra: Bananas, parsnips, yellow peppers, yellow beans, lemons, and sweet corn

Heart chakra: Green vegetables, apples, pears, green grapes, and kiwi fruit

Throat chakra: Plums, passion fruit, and blueberries

Brow chakra: Blackberries, radishes, and black currants

Crown chakra: Pale-colored peaches or melons

COLORING WITH DÉCOR AND CLOTHING

Never decorate a baby's room in bright colors; doing so would cause the baby to absorb the color and the energies within the color, and not be able to sleep. Use pastel shades, especially pale green, which many traditions consider good for growth and development.

If you find it hard to sleep, change your décor and bedclothes to something pale and restful. If you want a peaceful day spent puttering around the house or backyard, wear boring colors, but if you want to stand out, wear very bright colors. Black can be dramatic, but team it with something bright or something with an interesting pattern to give you an edge.

The Colors

Red is associated with the base chakra, so any part of the body from the base of the spine and genital area down to the soles of the feet would benefit from this color. If a higher chakra is functioning badly, red will help to clear and energize it. Red will enliven a body that has become sluggish and make it more active, so this could be good for someone whose lungs are congested, or perhaps someone whose mental processes have become slow. Red will give life to any bodily organ that isn't working efficiently, while on a psychological level, red gives strength and endows courage. Red is a great color to use if any of the upper chakras aren't working properly, but it would be a poor choice for someone who is angry or aggressive, as it would exacerbate the problem.

Orange is related to the sacral chakra, so it is useful for any ailment in the abdominal area, especially for bladder and hip problems. This chakra also relates to personal and sexual relationships. However, if the heart chakra is unwell, try orange healing, as it will help.

Green is related to the heart chakra, although some people see this area as two chakras, with one above the other. In that case, green is best suited to the upper of the two heart chakras. This color is specifically associated with the heart and chest area, but it can be used to cool and comfort the sacral area as well. Green is related to growth, security, regeneration, and earth energy.

Yellow is related to the solar plexus chakra, and to the person's willpower and "get up and go." It is concerned with ailments in the central area of the body, such as the stomach, kidneys, liver, and pancreas, especially if any of those organs need energizing. It is particularly suitable to those who work with their mind and intellect, and it can give clarity to those whose thinking is confused. If the client finds it difficult to think through a tricky problem, try using yellow healing against the throat or brow chakra.

Pink is the color most associated with love and affection, and for those who use the dual heart chakra system, this rules the lower of the two. It brings an enlivening energy due to the red that is part of the pink, and it also brings a peaceful and pure energy due to the white element in the color. Pink can help someone who is suffering psychological heartache, or it might be useful for heart trouble, lung problems, or stomach ulcers.

Light blue and **turquoise blue** are associated with the throat chakra and, therefore, with listening and talking—and communicating in general. If someone is suffering from ear, nose, or throat problems, blue healing might help. However, if the person is having problems in learning, communicating, listening, or even wishes to become clairaudient—which means to be able to hear on a spiritual level—blue healing might be too slow, so try yellow or even red healing. Blue is a calming color that brings peace, so it may be a good idea to line it up next to the base, sacral, or solar plexus chakra to calm an angry or anxious client and ease his mind. It is also said to be useful for an upset stomach or an ailing spleen.

Purple is the color of spirituality, so if someone is struggling with this aspect of life, this color will help. It can be used to ease base or solar plexus problems, such as anger or a lack of spirituality, or to help someone who has worldly success but wonders about the point of it all.

White is linked to purity, protection, and love, so if your client feels threatened, use lots of white color and bring down white light from the universe to give him healing. White rules some of the upper chakras that reach up from the person's aura to the heavens, although some systems associate this color with the crown chakra.

Gold is related to the chakra directly above the head, as it sits about six to nine inches above the crown of the head. Gold is said to be helpful for skeletal problems and anything else in the body of a hard nature, such as the skull, teeth, and nails. This color is obviously linked to spirituality and can help a person who is working on his mediumistic or spiritual gifts.

Other traditions give the chakras that are above the body color connections as follows:

Black	Eighth chakra	Black is a protective color.
Gold	Ninth chakra	Gold is a color of success and joy.
Brown	Tenth chakra	Brown is a practical, earthy color.
Pink	Eleventh chakra	Pink is a mix of vibrant red and spiritual white.
Indigo	Twelfth chakra	Indigo is a color that links to the sky and the universe.

Color Healing Chakras

Color healing is a way of introducing color to the chakras to produce a specific outcome. The colored objects could be pieces of ribbon, large buttons, marbles, pieces of card, painted stones, or perhaps scraps of material. Anything will work as long as the colors are bright, clear, and strong—and they must be plain rather than patterned.

With your client lying down comfortably, you place the colored item *alongside* his body, in line with the chakra or chakras that you wish to heal. This removes the necessity of putting anything directly *on* the client's body. Alternatively, your client can sit up and hold the colored object in his hand while you focus your healing energy on the chakra that needs help. Another method is to buy a number of inexpensive scarves or pieces of lightweight cloth and drape these around a seated client.

You can use the color that rules a particular chakra, on a "like for like" basis, such as yellow on yellow, or blue on blue, and so on, which would clear a serious blockage and get the chakra moving again. However, you could use "opposing" colors, such as a bright color against a sluggish upper chakra to cheer it up, or you could choose cooler colors, such as blue, green, or white, to calm down an overanxious person by placing it next to his solar plexus chakra.

Much of color healing will be a matter of intuition, but you can also check out the physical and psychological problems related to the chakras by reading chapter 10. If the person reacts in a way that surprises you or if he gets upset in any way, stop and offer him some water to drink and try again with a different color/chakra combination.

Once you have your colored item in place, you should give spiritual or energy healing by imagining energy coming down from the universe, taking note of the color that you are using and directing the energy to the client's chakra. Like much in the field of energy or spiritual healing, this will help the body to heal itself, but it would be unrealistic to expect a miracle cure.

When you have finished your work, thank your spiritual guides, close your own chakras, and wash your hands to remove any unwanted debris from the person you were attempting to heal.

Distant Color Healing Methods for Chakras

It is possible to give color healing at a distance. If you want to try this, tell your client to think of you at a specific time of the day, and when the time comes, quickly open your own chakras and tune in mentally to the client. Then think of the color, concentrate on it, and mentally direct it to the recipient. So, if your client is feeling washed out, you could send yellow, orange, or red, but if he is overwrought, try sending blue, purple, or green.

Energy healing works perfectly well over a distance, so distant color healing can be fun with which to experiment. For instance, you could try this experiment with a friend who has a particular illness: send the relevant color for the chakra that links with the ailment and ask your friend if he "picks up" the color. It's worth a try.

9

ESSENTIAL OILS FOR CHAKRAS

It is advisable to consult a qualified aromatherapist for the best treatment of chakra issues with essential oils, because oils can have a profound effect on the body. You should at least take advice from someone who knows what they are doing. It is best to avoid using essential oils on someone who is seriously unwell or pregnant. If using oils directly on the body, they must be diluted in carrier oil, but an alternative is to put a drop or two in a bath and bathe in the mixture. Or you can use a diffuser, which is a pottery holder that has room for a tea-light candle inside, with a little dish above to hold a few drops of oil. As the oil warms up, it evaporates and wafts around the room.

You can check out the nature of the chakras and the physical or emotional problems that are associated with each of them. Then you will be in a good position to choose an essential oil that will strengthen a weak chakra, calm down an overactive one, or improve general health and mood.

A Must

······◆◆◆◆◆◆······

Always try a patch test, whereby you put a tiny bit of the essential oil on the inner surface of your arm to see whether you get an allergic reaction. If you do, then that oil is not for you.

Suitable Essential Oils for the Chakras

Some oils work for more than one chakra, as you will see from the lists below.
It's worth noting that lavender and rose will help every chakra, especially if you
need more peace and love in your life.

Base Chakra	Sacral Chakra	Solar Plexus
• Oak Moss • Patchouli • Vetiver • Cedarwood • Ginger • Jasmine	• Clary sage • Jasmine • Cinnamon • Rose • Citrus • Geranium • Ginger	• Bergamot • Geranium • Ginger • Grapefruit • Juniper • Lemon • Peppermint • Rosemary • Coriander

Heart Chakra	Throat Chakra	Brow Chakra	Crown Chakra
• Bergamot • Rose • Ylang-ylang • Lemongrass • Aniseed • Basil • Ginger • Lavender • Myrrh	• Rosemary • Chamomile • Frankincense • Sandalwood • Geranium • Aniseed • Basil • Clary sage • Lavender	• Hyacinth • Geranium • Pine • Sage • Rose • Everlasting • Frankincense • Jasmine • Rosemary • Sandalwood	• Frankincense • Myrrh • Bay laurel • Lavender • Valerian • Jasmine • Cedarwood • Chamomile • Frankincense • Jasmine • Neroli

A Quick-Fix List for Common Conditions

Chakra	Weakness	Essential Oil
Base	Low self-esteem	Vetiver
Sacral	Oversensitive	Jasmine
Solar Plexus	Fearful	Ginger
Heart	Feeling rejection	Rose
Throat	Can't get others to listen or understand	Lavender
Brow	Disorganized	Sandalwood
Crown	Exhausted	Frankincense

10

HEALING EMOTIONAL PAIN THROUGH CHAKRAS

There are thousands of emotional and psychological situations that plague us, but we can focus on only a few obvious ones here. For instance, worry is a common emotion, and it stems from fear, which may be well-founded or due to an overactive imagination. Either way, the best treatment is to visualize bright yellow light coming down from the universe and pouring into the solar plexus chakra, because this will increase courage. Meanwhile, it would also be a great idea to put an imaginary shield on the front and back of the central area of the body in order to protect the solar plexus chakra from attack by outside forces. Financial loss and poverty are hard to cope with, but healing to the base chakra can help, while healing to the brow chakra can help a person think clearly.

Other people sometimes upset us, but healing to the sacral and heart chakras gives us the strength to cope with their bad behavior or, if needed, the courage to walk away from them. Well-aligned throat and brow chakras help us think clearly, listen carefully, and say the right words. If you are angry about something, you can easily treat this one yourself. Ask your preferred deity or spiritual guide to send cooling and calming spiritual healing to your base, sacral, and solar plexus chakras.

This chapter will go through each of the chakras, their most common problems, and how to heal them.

Base Chakra

POTENTIAL PROBLEMS

The base chakra is about survival, so at the most fundamental level, this means having enough clean water, food, clothing, shelter, and the means to stay alive and healthy. In our world, it is best to move away from physical danger even if it means walking out on a relationship or moving to a different area. If you are at some event when someone bothers you, look as if you are going to the restroom, call a cab, and slip out the back way. *Never* get into a car, house, or some other place with someone about whom you feel uneasy. Sustained bullying is harmful to the recipient's mental health, so he must move away from the person who is bullying him, or find some way of putting an end to the bully's activities if that is possible.

Another problem is perfectionism, whereby the individual punishes himself for not doing everything perfectly. This is a losing battle, so the subject has to accept that everyone messes things up from time to time and that he is no different from anyone else in this respect.

SIMPLE HEALING METHODS

Every now and then, the subject should lie down quietly somewhere and meditate for a while. He should try to leave the past behind and give up worrying about the future, while focusing on the good things in his life. He should count his blessings, if possible. He should hold a piece of blue lace agate or turquoise in his hand while imagining white light flecked with blue and pale green coming down and giving him whole-body healing. Then he should allow pale blue light to pour into his base chakra. He should relax and even take a nap if possible.

Sacral Chakra

POTENTIAL PROBLEMS

The sacral chakra is associated with sex and with close personal relationships, and we all know there is plenty that can go wrong here. A classic situation is living with someone who is suspicious and jealous for no reason, and if this drifts into the area of emotional/ psychological abuse or physical violence, it has nothing to do with love and everything to do with the other person's need to hurt and control others. The answer is to move on as soon as it is practical to do so. The same goes for a partner who is taking advantage of the subject, or a partner whose interests take precedence over the needs of the subject.

Other problems arise when the individual ignores his intuition and lets situations take hold that should have been sidestepped earlier. This person should accept that he isn't superman and take more notice of his intuition the next time a similar situation arises.

SIMPLE HEALING METHODS

The individual should relax and meditate by bringing down white light with healing pale blue or turquoise flecks of light in it. He should start by letting this drift over his whole body and then pour a concentrated dose into his sacral chakra. He could hold a piece of healing turquoise in his hands while doing this meditation.

Solar Plexus Chakra

POTENTIAL PROBLEMS

If the subject is being pushed around and disrespected by others, it is no good for his mental and physical health. He must avoid being bullied by others, but he must also refrain from doing the bullying himself. He needs to stand up for himself but not to overdo it by being mean or hurting others. It is never a good idea to give away one's money or goods in order to be liked, and the subject should not let others take advantage of him. The solar plexus chakra rules self-esteem, self-respect, and personal power, so the person mustn't succumb to envy of those who are better off than he is nor want what he can't have. This person may find learning a struggle.

SIMPLE HEALING METHODS

The individual must look after his health, appearance, and diet and he needs to exercise regularly, even if this is only going for a walk, as this will raise his spirits and improve his health.

Meditations that are designed to help the subject dump troublesome people or walk away from hopeless situations can help. A useful one is for the subject to imagine a large plastic bag and to visualize himself throwing his problems into the bag and, when the bag is full, tying it up, putting it on a bonfire, and getting rid of it all. A color meditation might also help. This involves the person imagining yellow light coming down and surrounding him, and then an extra boost of light pouring into the solar plexus chakra. Or he could hold a piece of citrine and let its energy pour into him.

Heart Chakra

POTENTIAL PROBLEMS

This is the stuff of novels and films about star-crossed lovers, which goes to show just how important this area of life is to all of us. It is also a fact that in many relationships, one person does the loving while the other is on the receiving end of that love—for good or ill.

So, if the individual finds himself with a selfish, unloving, or hurtful partner, the only thing to do is to move away from the situation and find someone worthy of his love. If the partner is lying, cheating, or using the individual, this relationship is obviously not going to work out in the end. Some of the problem might stem from a lack of self-esteem on the part of the subject.

SIMPLE HEALING METHODS

There are many courses that teach self-esteem and skills for coping with relationships or improving them. Others teach the individual how to respect himself and others, and even how to become more lovable. Some people need to work on themselves, such as improving their grooming habits or taking measures to become healthier.

A good heart meditation would be to lie down and imagine white light flecked with green light pouring down to calm the heart chakra. If the person's love life is nonexistent or boring, he should try a meditation that is a combination of white light and orange flecks. The person could try this while holding a piece of jade for love, or a piece of carnelian or jasper if he wants more passion in his life.

Throat Chakra

POTENTIAL PROBLEMS

This chakra is associated with communication problems that might include not listening to others or not taking enough notice of what is going on at work or at home. The subject may find it hard to express himself or to make others listen to him, so they may not know how he feels. He may be reluctant to speak up when something upsets him but quick to come out with unpleasant remarks or to say hurtful things to others. He may be unrealistic, fussy, or just plain difficult, or he may be with someone else who is like this.

SIMPLE HEALING METHODS

There are so many common problems related to communication and this is the chakra most often in need of healing. The person who needs this healing could meditate on how he wants life to be and could then start to work toward that objective. A color meditation would involve bringing down white light, with a little pale blue to calm the chakra. If the chakra needs a boost, a white light meditation with some flecks of yellow would help with personal empowerment and also with learning difficulties. If the person can do this while holding a piece of citrine, this would boost the effects of the meditation.

Brow Chakra

POTENTIAL PROBLEMS

This chakra is associated with intuition and ego. An individual who sacrifice too much or can't stand up for himself might have an issue here. He is angered or upset easily, and his mind often goes back to unpleasant memories, replaying them over and over again. He might be lonely and isolated, afraid of getting hurt again.

SIMPLE HEALING METHODS

Chakra healing to this area can help people become more able and more confident. It can also aid the development of intuition, sensitivity, and ability to channel or link to spirit. Crystal healing is probably the best treatment. The subject could hold a piece of amethyst or sodalite in his hand and ask for the energies to be released into his body.

Crown Chakra

POTENTIAL PROBLEMS

The crown chakra rules the link to spirit and the first slight glimmering of the next world. This will need healing if the person is too interested in religion and spiritual matters for common sense to apply.

SIMPLE HEALING METHODS

The individual should hold a piece of blue lace agate in each hand and imagine calming green and blue light entering the crystal. Then he should let the crystal release its energies into his hands, which will help him regain balance and common sense.

✳ ✳ ✳

11

MAGICAL AND MEDITATIVE CHAKRA TECHNIQUES

The chakra-healing ideas in this chapter come from the world of magic and Wicca. The first spell works by focusing the mind on the problem and its solution, and sending the thoughts out to the universe. This might help alleviate a physical problem, but it could also help to banish unhappiness or turn a bad situation round.

Create an Altar

Oddly enough, the best place to create an altar is the kitchen, because the electrical equipment in the vicinity seems to give a boost to magical spells. Plus, candles will be used, and usually kitchens don't have curtains or upholstered furniture that can catch fire.

Find a large tray—you can even use a metal baking tray—and cover it with a clean cloth. The following lists show some essential items to put on the tray and others that are optional.

Essentials

- Something that represents the person or the problem. This could be hospital paperwork, a job application, a bank statement, a photo of a person, or a love letter. If you are giving healing to yourself, put your own photo on the altar.
- A candleholder for a tall candle or a tea-light candle—either will do.
- An incense stick or diffuser with a very small amount of the essential oil of the your choice.
- Some pieces of paper and several colored pens.
- A little dish with some salt in it.
- A little bowl with some spring water or collected rainwater in it.
- Matches or a lighter on hand.

Options

- A selection of crystals if you have any.
- An essential oil if you have one.
- Ribbons or beads of various colors.
- A relevant tarot card.

- A relevant rune stone.
- A piece of jewelry or an object that
  means something to you.

The Method

- Set the dish of salt (earth) and spring
  or rainwater on the tray.
- Find a candle or tea-light in the appropriate color per the chart below
  and set it in place.
- Set the incense stick or essential oil in place.
- Take your paper and pens and choose the right color for the chakra that
  you wish to heal. Here is the color list for reference and a very basic
  description of problems that can occur with each chakra:

Chakra	Candle Color	Meaning
Base	Red	Fear of financial disaster, bowel and genital area
Sacral	Orange	Relationship or sexual problem, reproductive area
Solar Plexus	Yellow	Being pushed around by others, digestive organ area
Heart	Green	Lack of love, heart and lung area
Throat	Pale blue or turquoise	Can't get point across to others or understand what they are on about, throat, neck and ear area Lack of love, heart and lung area
Brow	Deep blue	Lack of sense in self or others, toothache, headaches
Crown	Purple	Spirituality being blocked, lack of compassion in others
Higher chakras	White or gold	Fear of life, fear of death, vague fears

- Write down exactly what you want the spell to achieve. This doesn't have to be in the form of poetry, and neither do you need to end it with words such as "so mote it be" although you can do these things if you feel like it. Don't write a whole shopping list of desires; just stick to one thing for the moment.
- Put the letter, photo, or whatever you have selected to represent the predicament on the tray.
- If you want to add a tarot card, rune, or something else of the kind, do so.
- If you want to add some crystals to bring about the healing you need, add these now.
- If you want to add colored ribbons, beads, buttons, and so on in colors that represent what you are trying to achieve, add them now. These can be in a variety of colors if that's what you want to do.
- Light the candle and the incense or diffuser. The candle represents fire and the incense or oil represents air.
- Read the spell three times and then wave it through the incense.
- Wave the letter, photo, and paper with your message on it through the incense.
- Read what you wrote three times and put the paper on the tray.
- The incense stick will soon burn down, although the essence will keep going for a while longer. The candle will take longest, but you must let it burn down all the way.
- When the candle has burned out, use your matches to carefully burn the paper with the spell. Do this in the sink and wash the ash down the drain.
- Throw the salt and water onto a bit of paper towel and throw out the candle stump or the tea-light holder.
- Thank your guides, angels, deity, and the universe.

Wait for things to change for the better. It might take a month or two for this to happen, as it sometimes requires a shift in the position of the moon or Mercury before things change for the better.

Meditation with Candle Power

Candle meditation is a wonderful way to meditate, especially if you have never tried meditation before, as concentrating on the candle flame will put you in the right headspace. Lighting a candle creates the right ambience and provides something to focus on. While looking at the flame of the candle, you clear your mind, and the more you concentrate on the flame, the easier it is to keep other thoughts from entering your mind. This makes it quicker and easier for you to connect with the universe before meditating on your particular choice of topic.

The colors link to the chakras as follows, and so you can use this guide to select the color candle you are going to meditate with:

Color	Chakra	Intention or Desired Result
Black	Base	Destroys any negative energy around you, gives protection, heals past hurts
Brown	Base	Grounding, regaining balance
Red	Base	Sexuality, passion, courage
Orange	Sacral	Good for legal matters and finance
Yellow	Solar plexus	Mental clarity, clairvoyance, confidence
Green	Heart	Love, compassion, luck
Pink	Heart	Love and harmony, friendships
Blue	Throat	Opens the lines of communication for inspiration, happiness, and forgiveness
Dark blue	Brow	Connects you to higher self and psychic awareness
White	Crown	Brings peace, clarity, and truth
Silver	Crown and above	Releases negativity and aids psychic development
Gold	Crown and above	Connects to spirit world, also helps heal past-life issues

- Light the candle and sit down.
- Close your eyes and relax.
- Breathe regularly and fairly deeply.
- Imagine yourself walking along an open area of grass or sand.
- See a big bag into which you can put your troubles.
- Put your troubles in the bag and imagine it going far away into the universe.
- See the benefits that you want to have in your life materializing in front of you.
- Open your eyes, focus on the candlelight, and ask for the help that you need.
- Slowly come back to this world.
- If it is safe to do so, leave the candle to burn down; if not, put it out.
- Thank your deity, angels, higher consciousness, and the universe.

Other Forms of Magic and Meditation

Many methods of using magic and meditation to help heal chakras and ailments have been developed over the centuries and around the world. Here are just a few.

Shamanism

The Kalahari Bushmen of Namibia are the only humans whose DNA stretches back over many millennia without being mingled with any other human type, so not only are they the purest type of human being but they are our ancestors as well. Let us now look at how things have been conducted over a period of at least 35,000 years and how they still are.

A shaman (healer) dances to the sound of drumming until he slips into a trance state, then he taps into help from ancestors who have passed over, and these ancestors show him exactly what is wrong with the patient. The shaman then feels himself being taken over by the spirit of a cheetah—an animal whose spirit is considered to have great healing powers—after which the shaman directs energy to the relevant parts of the patient's body.

There are shamans in many cultures around the world, and the methods they use are much the same the world over. It isn't far removed from energy healing, Reiki, or spiritual healing, so it probably works on the body's regenerative powers in much the same way. Shamanic healing can be directed to the relevant chakras.

Affirmations

Many people find affirmations useful for emotional problems such as low self-esteem or being upset after a relationship comes to an end. You can buy a book of affirmations, look them up on the internet, or make up your own affirmations, then write them down and repeat them every day. Light a candle in the appropriate chakra color to help you.

The Seven Rays

The Seven Rays system is an extremely esoteric spiritual system linked to the ascended masters, to God, and to Jesus. It was either discovered, or perhaps rediscovered from ancient origins, by the Theosophists, and can be linked to the chakra system or to astrology. This system can identify issues related to health, personality, and psychology and suggest ways of healing them.

Heart Healing

Some healers believe there is a method that sends energy directly out from their own heart chakra, but this kind of healing requires a great deal of unconditional love, and not everyone is able to give it.

Meditations from Ancient Times

These two ancient meditation techniques direct energy to the chakras of someone you wish to heal, but you need to choose the right depending on the person's particular astrological requirements.

The first meditation, "gold healing," is suitable for people born under fire and air signs, and it works by bringing energy down from the universe into the crown chakra, after which the healing works its way downward through the chakra system.

The second, "green healing," is suitable for those born under earth and water signs and it travels upward from the earth, through the feet and upward through the chakra system.

Fire signs: Aries, Leo, Sagittarius

Air signs: Gemini, Libra, Aquarius

Earth signs: Taurus, Virgo, Capricorn

Water signs: Cancer, Scorpio, Pisces

Gold Healing

This method is suitable for fire and air sign people. It brings healing energy down from above, through the chakras. It is like tapping into the power of the sun.

PREPARATION

You need to prepare yourself before this healing session, and this is how you do it:

- There is an eighth chakra that sits above the head, and this is gold in color—a bit like a small sun—so that is your starting point.
- Imagine the sun chakra growing in size and intensity until it is really glowing.
- Now visualize your crown chakra opening and see a great shaft of golden light from this sun entering your body through your crown chakra.
- Let the light fill your entire body, including your surrounding aura and the area below your feet.

- You may become conscious of a golden glow in and around you.
- Feel the light running down your arms and gathering in your hands as if it can't wait to get out and do its work.
- Now you are ready to give the healing.

Healing Session

- Ask your client to sit in a chair with his back to you.
- Stand a few feet away from your client and hold your hands out toward him.
- Keep your hands about six inches apart and release the healing power gathering up in the palms of your hands and let it flow out to your client.
- At this point, you may become aware of blockages in one or another of your client's chakras, so focus on sending healing to the blocked chakra, or to any other part of the client's body that seems to be out of sorts.
- When you feel that you have done enough, bring your hands down and let your eighth chakra calm down again.
- Relax and thank your spiritual guides and helpers.
- Wash your hands.

Green Healing

This method is suitable for earth and water sign people. It brings healing energy up from the earth through the chakras. In this case, the energy is like the flow of the sea. This healing will switch off if you touch your client, so keep your hands about six inches away from the client at all times.

PREPARATION

You need to prepare yourself before this healing session, and this is how you do it:

- The energy source is the earth below, so imagine green light entering your body via the chakras in the soles of your feet.
- Let the light fill your entire body, including your surrounding aura and above your head.
- You may become conscious of a green light filling your body, your aura, and above your head.
- Feel the light running down your arms and gathering in your hands as if it can't wait to get out and do its work.
- Now you are ready to give healing.

Healing Session

- Ask your client to sit in a chair with his back to you.
- Stand a few feet away from your client and hold your hands out toward him.
- Keep your hands about six inches apart and release the healing power gathering up in the palms of your hands and let it flow out to your client.
- Now approach your client and place your hands on either side of his shoulders, about six inches away.
- Run your hands up and down the aura in his arms and shoulders, giving green healing as you go.
- At this point, you may become aware of blockages in one or another of your client's chakras, so focus on sending healing to the blocked chakra, or to any other part of the client's body that seems to be out of sorts.
- Now raise your hands so that they are at either side of your client's head, and then bring them to the top of his head, but avoid touching your client. As you reach the head, especially the crown of the head, imagine the green light turning purple.
- Keep giving healing until you feel that you have done enough, then step back and end the session.
- Relax and thank your spiritual guides and helpers.
- Wash your hands.

12

CHAKRA HEALING FOR ANIMALS

Do animals have chakras? Well, animals have feelings and they know how to love. In addition to this, I and many other mediums often find it easier to link to the spirit of an animal that has passed over than to a human. Animals are God's creatures and they are part of our world, so to anybody with even the slightest interest in spirituality, it seems obvious that they have chakras, just as humans do.

All vertebrate animals have a spine, and that is where you will find the seven main chakras. In a pet such as a dog or a cat, it is easy to work out where these are, as they line up with the bodily organs in the same way as they do for humans. However, let us say that you are worried about your pet python; you'll have to make a sketch of the snake and then dowse the reptile with a pendulum, noting the chakra positions on the sketch as you find them. As you run the pendulum over the body of the creature, ask your guides to show you where the crown chakra is situated, then the brow chakra, and so on.

The activity of the chakras is the same for animals as it is for humans—up to a point . . .

Important Advice

It's best to consult the right kind of vet to diagnose and treat a sick animal, but chakra healing can give an extra boost that will help the creature's body to heal itself. In addition, the extra love and attention that you give the animal will help it feel better. I think this must go for a working animal or a farm animal as much as for a much-loved pet.

Once you know what is ailing your animal, you may be able to work out which of the chakras needs to be healed. If your pet is just a bit off and you don't think it necessary to take it to the vet for a diagnosis, you can probably figure out which of the chakras needs healing.

The Seven Main Chakras

BASE CHAKRA

Just as this is concerned with survival in humans, so it is with animals. It also rules the lower end of the body and the adrenal glands.

SACRAL CHAKRA

The sacral chakra rules the reproductive organs and sexual activity.

SOLAR PLEXUS CHAKRA

This chakra is connected to the central organs of the body, such as the pancreas and liver. It also rules willpower or lack of it.

HEART CHAKRA

The heart chakra rules the lungs and heart but also love, affection, and sometimes even hatred.

THROAT CHAKRA

This chakra is concerned with the throat and neck, but it allows the creature to communicate its needs and feelings to other animals and to us.

BROW CHAKRA

The brow chakra is associated with intuition and fear but also with the ears and the facial features.

CROWN CHAKRA

If the animal is aware of the spiritual world, that awareness would be centered in this chakra; otherwise, it relates to the brain and thinking process.

Finding Weak Chakras

Take a pendulum and slowly work your way along your animal's spine, asking the pendulum to react when it meets a chakra that is too open or misaligned. Then ask the pendulum to react when a chakra is blocked, and be prepared to give this more healing than those that are too open or misaligned.

Healing

Energy Healing

You can use any kind of energy healing on an animal. I've seen it done and it works surprisingly quickly.

Crystal Healing

When the animal is resting, place crystals that are appropriate to the chakras nearby, but not so near that the animal can get at them and swallow them. Send a bit of white light down to the crystals and the animal while you are doing so. Stay with the animal while you are using the crystals, and when you finish, put the crystals in a bag and remove them from the area.

Essential Oils

There are people who use essences on animals, but I don't think it's a good idea. Whether placed on or near the creature, burned in a diffuser, or even burned as an incense stick, the material could upset the animal and make things worse.

Magnet Therapy

Magnets can be very helpful for a sick animal, especially for one with rheumatism. Include a magnet in a leash or bridle, or leave magnets near the spot where the animal rests—but not where it could get at them and swallow them.

✳ ✳ ✳

APPENDIX: CHAKRA CONNECTIONS

Here is a list of the connections, links, or correspondences for each chakra.

CHAKRA	BASE	SACRAL	SOLAR PLEXUS	HEART
POSITION	Base of the spine	Abdomen through to the sacral spine	Above the naval through to central spine	Central chest through to the spine
MAIN ROLE	Survival, life	Creation, emotions	Energy, control, belief	Love, relating, respect, creativity
BODILY AREA	Legs, base of the spine	Reproductive organs, bowels	Digestion	Heart, lungs, upper digestive tract
GLAND	Adrenal	Ovaries, testes	Pancreas, endocrine	Thymus
SENSE	Smell	Taste	Sight	Touch
VEDIC NAME	Muladhara	Svadhistana	Manipura	Anahata
OTHER NAMES	Root chakra, red chakra	Spleen chakra, orange chakra	Yellow chakra, naval chakra	Green chakra
NUMBER	The first chakra	The second chakra	The third chakra	The fourth chakra
COLOR	Red	Orange	Yellow	Green
GENDER	Yang, masculine, positive	Yin, feminine, negative	Yang, masculine, positive	Yin, feminine, negative
ANIMAL	Elephant	Crocodile	Ram	Wolf
LOTUS PETALS	Four	Six	Ten	Twelve
SHAPE	Square	Crescent moon, pyramid	Circle	Cross
ELEMENT	Earth	Water	Fire	Air
PLANET	Mars	Moon	Sun	Venus
ZODIAC SIGN	Aries, Scorpio	Cancer	Leo	Taurus, Libra
MANTRA	Lam	Vam	Ram	Yam
MUSIC	Drumming	Strings	Reed, horn	Flute, woodwind instruments

CHAKRA	THROAT	BROW	CROWN
POSITION	The throat through to the nape of the neck	Central forehead just above the eyes	The crown of the head
MAIN ROLE	Communication	Knowledge, clarity	Spirituality
BODILY AREA	Throat	Head (facial area: eyes, skull)	Head, central nervous system (facial area: head)
GLAND	Thyroid, parathyroid	Pineal, pituitary	Pineal, pituitary
SENSE	Hearing	Sight	Oneness with the universe
VEDIC NAME	Vishuddha	Ajna	Sahasrara
OTHER NAMES	Light blue chakra	Third eye chakra, frontal chakra, indigo chakra	Violet chakra
NUMBER	The fifth chakra	The sixth chakra	The seventh chakra
COLOR	Sky blue	Indigo blue	Violet, purple, in some traditions white or gold
GENDER	Yang, masculine, positive	Yang, masculine, positive	Yin/Yang, thus masculine and feminine
ANIMAL	Eagle	Ancestors	Angels
LOTUS PETALS	Sixteen	A circle with a petal on each side	Purple lily or many petals
SHAPE	Cup	Star of David	Lotus, lily
ELEMENT	Air/Ether	Light	Light
PLANET	Mercury	Jupiter	Saturn
ZODIAC SIGN	Gemini, Virgo	Sagittarius, Pisces	Capricorn, Aquarius
MANTRA	Ham	Aum	Nnn
MUSIC	Singing	Sacred songs and music	Silence

CONCLUSION

So I end where I began this book, which is to say that you must use common sense when you fall ill, and go to your doctor, dentist, osteopath, optometrist, podiatrist, or whatever you need. However, you can use the methods in this book to give your chakras a boost and help your mind, body, and spirit with self-healing, or to give help and healing to someone else. Even in the worst case of knowing that someone close to you is dying, a bit of chakra healing will help to ease their passage. It is also worth it for the bereaved person to get some healing to help them cope.

I found writing this book fascinating, and I am well aware that it could have been twice the size, but I have tried to restrict it to methods that are useful, inexpensive, and easy to achieve. I hope you find the book helpful as time goes by.

Good luck,
Roberta Vernon

ABOUT THE AUTHOR

Roberta Vernon's grandmother was quite psychic and she was into dream interpretation. Her grandfather liked numerology and her mother was an amateur palmist, so it isn't surprising that Roberta would eventually take an interest in esoteric ideas. She took up palmistry at a young age, then got into psychology and astrology, and later became fascinated by the chakras, crystals, and various kinds of healing. Roberta lives in London, England, and she is married with children and grandchildren. Roberta's other book in this series is *In Focus: Palmistry.*

IMAGE CREDITS

INDEX

Affirmations, 128

Agate, blue lace, 101

Air element/signs, 71, 128

Altar, creating, 123–124

Alternative therapies, defined, 8. *See also specific therapies*

Amber, 100

Amethyst, 101

Animal connections of chakras, 136–137

Animals, chakra healing for, 133–135

Arm (elbow) chakras, 62, 64, 95

Astrology, chakras, elements and, 22, 70–71, 128

Aura
about: definition and description of, 15
chakras and, 15
color healing and, 106, 109
energy healing and, 8
feeling energy/pressure and, 77
gold healing and, 129, 131
Reiki healing and, 92

Base (or root) chakra, **25–30**
about: overview of functions and associations, 17–23
of animals, 134
balanced, 26–27
body and health associations, 29
checklist for identifying weaknesses, 68
color of and healing with color, 20, 108, 109
correspondences/ connections, 30, 136
crystals for clearing, 102
deficient or damaged, 28
details and key ideas, 25
elements and, 70
emotional pain/problems and healing methods, 117–118
essential oils for, 114, 115, 135
exaggerated, 28
flower images and number of petals, 17–19

money, business, and career factors, 27
as one of seven main chakras, 16
position of, 25
problems related to, 93
topics associated with, 25–26

Batch healing, 83

Behind-the-ears, chakras, 62, 63

Black color, 109, 124, 126

Blue, healing with, 108, 124, 126

Blue lace agate, 101

Body
main chakras, 16–19. *See also* Base (or root) chakra; Brow chakra ("third eye"); Crown chakra; Heart chakra; Sacral chakra; Solar plexus chakra; Throat chakra
minor chakras above, 61–63
minor chakras below, 65
minor chakras on, 62, 63–65
sketch, 74, 75

Body and health associations
base chakra, 29
brow chakra ("third eye"), 55
crown chakra, 58
heart chakra, 46
sacral chakra, 35
solar plexus chakra, 40
throat chakra, 50

Brow chakra ("third eye"), **52–55**
about: overview of functions and associations, 17–23
of animals, 134
balanced, 52–53
body and health associations, 55
checklist for identifying weaknesses, 69
color of, 20
correspondences/ connections, 55, 137
crystals for clearing, 103
deficient or damaged, 54
details and key ideas, 52
elements and, 71
emotional pain/problems and healing methods, 121

essential oils for, 114, 115, 135
exaggerated, 54
flower images and number of petals, 17–19
money, business, and career factors, 53
as one of seven main chakras, 16
position of, 52
problems related to, 94
topics associated with, 52

Brown color, 109, 126

Candles
affirmations and, 128
colored, for Wiccan spell, 124–125
meditation with candle power, 126–127

Career. *See* Money, business, and career factors

Carnelian, 100

Chakra healing. *See also* Colors, healing with; Crystal healing; Magic and meditation techniques; Reiki healing
for animals, 133–135
basics of. *See* Energy and spiritual healing
essential oils for, 113–115, 135
methods overview, 8–9
this book and, 7, 8–9, 138
warnings, 23

Chakras. *See also* Minor chakras; *specific chakras*
astrology and, 22, 70–71
aura and. *See* Aura
blocked, effects of, 15
body diagrams showing, 19, 62
closing, 87
colors of, 20, 136–137
defined, 13, 14–15
elements and, 70–71
flower images and number of petals, 17–19
functions and associations, 15, 17–19, 136–137
historical perspective, 13
kundalini and, 20–22, 26, 93

main (seven), 16
mind, intellect, ego and,
14–15
number and locations of, 16
opening, 86
physical body and, 14
problems related to, 93–94
problems with. *See*
Chakra healing; Energy
and spiritual healing;
Identifying weak chakras
psychology and, 23
religion and, 16
soul and, 23
spiritual nature and, 15
three levels of, 14–15
Clearing sluggish chakras,
102–103
Clear quartz, 100
Closing chakras, 87
Colors, healing with
basics of, 106
with clothing and décor, 107
colors and their associations,
107–109
colors of chakras and,
136–137
distant healing methods, 111
fruits, vegetables, and related
chakras, 106
healing chakras, 110–111
Complementary therapies. *See
also specific therapies*
about: overview of, 7
credential for practitioners
of, 105
defined, 8
how they work, 105
Crown chakra, **56–59**
about: overview of functions
and associations, 17–23
of animals, 134
balanced, 56
body and health associations,
58
checklist for identifying
weaknesses, 69
color of, 20
correspondences/
connections, 59, 137
crystals for clearing, 103
deficient or damaged, 58
details and key ideas, 56
emotional pain/problems
and healing methods, 121

essential oils for, 114, 115,
135
exaggerated, 57
flower images and number of
petals, 17–19
money, business, and career
factors, 57
as one of seven main
chakras, 16
position of, 56
problems related to, 94
topics associated with, 56
Crystal healing, 97–103
about: overview of, 97
for animals, 135
clearing sluggish chakras,
102–103
common problems and
crystals for, 100–101
crystals for, 100–101,
102–103
preparing crystals for, 97–98
procedure and guidelines, 99

Distance-healing, 83, 111
Doubled heart chakra, 62, 64
Dowsing rods, 76

Ears, chakras behind, 62, 63
Earth element/signs, 70, 128
Ego, chakra healing and, 88
Eighth chakra (money and
death), 61, 62, 69, 109,
129–130
Elbow. *See* Arm (elbow) chakras
Element connections of chakras,
136–137
Elements. *See* Astrology,
chakras, elements and
Eleventh chakra, 109
Emotional pain, healing,
117–121
Energy. *See also* Chakras; *specific
chakras*
chakras as centers of, 14
feeling, 77
healing with. *See* Chakra
healing
kundalini, 20–22, 26, 93
weaknesses. *See* Identifying
weak chakras
Energy and spiritual healing.
See also Chakra healing;
Colors, healing with; Crystal
healing; Magic and meditation

techniques; Reiki healing
about: overview of, 83
for animals, 133–135
batch healing, 83
closing chakras, 87
defined, 8
at a distance, 83, 111
doing no harm, 89
ego and, 88
essential oils for, 113–115, 135
guidelines and steps, 83–89
how it works, 84–85
important points to
remember, 89
lessons, 88
opening chakras, 86
as a profession, 87–89
safety precaution, 89
setting your intention, 89
spirituality and, 85
when you have finished, 87
Essential oils for chakras,
113–115, 135

Female figure, 75
Finger chakras, 62, 64
Fire element/signs, 70, 128
Flower images and number of
petals, 17–19
Foot chakras, 62, 65, 95
Forehead chakra, 62, 63
Fruits, color of, chakras and, 106

Gender of chakras, 136–137
Gland connections of chakras,
136–137
Gold, healing with, 109, 124,
126, 129–130
Green, healing with, 108, 124,
126, 130–131
Ground chakras, 62, 65

Hand (palm) chakras, 62, 64, 95
Healing. *See* Chakra healing;
Identifying weak chakras
Heart chakra, **42–46**. *See also*
Doubled heart chakra
about: overview of functions
and associations, 17–23
of animals, 134
balanced, 43–44
body and health associations,
46
checklist for identifying
weaknesses, 68

color of and healing with
colors, 20, 108
correspondences/
connections, 46, 136
crystals for clearing, 103
deficient or damaged, 45
details and key ideas, 42
elements and, 70, 71
emotional pain/problems
and healing methods,
119–120
essential oils for, 114, 115,
135
exaggerated, 44–45
flower images and number of
petals, 17–19
money, business, and career
factors, 44
as one of seven main
chakras, 16
position of, 42
problems related to, 93
topics associated with, 42–43
Heart healing, 128
Hip chakras, 62, 65

Identifying weak chakras, 66–79
of animals, 134
astrology, elements and,
70–71
checklist for, 68–69
with dowsing rods, 76
feeling energy and, 77
general guidelines for, 67
malfunctioning chakra
identifiers, 76
marking troubled chakras,
73, 74–75
with pendulum, 72–77, 134
pinpointing malfunctioning
chakra, 76
quiz for, 78–79
Indigo color, 109
Intention, setting, 89

Jade, 120
Jasper, red, 101, 120

Knee chakras, 62, 65, 95
Kundalini, 20–22, 26, 93

Lessons, for chakra healing, 88
Lotus petals of chakras, 136–137

Magic and meditation
techniques, 123–131

affirmations, 128
altar for, 123–124
gold healing, 129–130
green healing, 130–131
heart healing, 128
meditation from ancient
times, 128
meditation with candle
power, 126–127
the Seven Rays, 128
shamanism, 127
Wiccan method, 123–125
Magnet therapy, 135
Main chakras. See Base (or root)
chakra; Brow chakra ("third
eye"); Crown chakra; Heart
chakra; Sacral chakra; Solar
plexus chakra; Throat chakra
Male figure, 74
Mantra connections of chakras,
136–137
Meditation. See Magic and
meditation techniques
Meridians, chakras and, 13
Minor chakras. See also Eighth
chakra; Eleventh chakra;
Ninth chakra; Tenth chakra
above the body, 61–63
below the body, 65
on the body, 62, 63–65. See
also specific chakras
diagram showing locations, 62
Reiki and, 95
Money, business, and career
factors
base chakra, 27
brow chakra ("third eye"), 53
crown chakra, 57
heart chakra, 44
sacral chakra, 33–34
solar plexus chakra, 38–39
throat chakra, 48–49
Music connections of chakras,
136–137

Names (other) of chakras,
136–137
Ninth chakra (causes and
soapboxes), 62, 63, 109
Number of each chakra, 62, 63,
136–137

Obsidian, 101
Oils, essential, for chakras,
113–115, 135
Opening chakras, 86

Orange, healing with, 108, 124,
126

Palm chakras. See Hand (palm)
chakras
Pelvic chakras, 62, 65
Pendulum, finding chakra
problems with, 72–77, 134
Pets, chakra healing for,
133–135
Pink, healing with, 108, 109, 126
Planet connections of chakras,
136–137
Position of chakras, 136–137
Problems. See Chakra healing;
Energy and spiritual healing;
Identifying weak chakras
Psychological/emotional pain,
healing, 117–121
Psychology, chakras and, 23
Purple, healing with, 109, 124

Quartz, clear, rose, and
amethyst, 100, 101
Quiz, for identifying weak
chakras, 78–79

Red, healing with, 108, 124, 126
Red jasper, 101, 120
Reiki healing, 91–95
chakras and, 93–94, 95
healing chakras, 94–95
masters of, 92
minor chakras and, 95
procedure and guidelines,
91–92, 94–95
Religion, chakras and, 16
Roles of chakras, 136–137. See
also specific chakras
Rose quartz, 100

Sacral chakra, **31–36**
about: overview of functions
and associations, 17–23
of animals, 134
balanced, 32–33
body and health associations,
35
checklist for identifying
weaknesses, 68
color of and healing with
color, 20, 108
correspondences/
connections, 36, 136
crystals for clearing, 102
deficient or damaged, 34–35

details and key ideas, 31
elements and, 70, 71
emotional pain/problems
and healing methods, 118
essential oils for, 114, 115,
135
exaggerated, 34
flower images and number of
petals, 17–19
money, business, and career
factors, 33–34
as one of seven main
chakras, 16
position of, 31
problems related to, 93
topics associated with, 31–32
Safety precaution, 89
Sense connections of chakras,
136–137
The Seven Rays, 128
Shamanism, 127
Shape of chakras, 136–137
Shoulder chakras, 62, 63, 95
Side chakra, 62, 64
Silver, 126
Snowflake obsidian, 101
Sodalite, 101
Solar plexus chakra, **37–41**
about: overview of functions
and associations, 17–23
of animals, 134
balanced, 38
body and health associations,
40
checklist for identifying
weaknesses, 68
color of and healing with
color, 20, 108
correspondences/
connections, 41, 136
crystals for clearing, 102
deficient or damaged, 39–40
details and key ideas, 37
elements and, 70, 71
emotional pain/problems
and healing methods, 119
essential oils for, 114, 115,
135
exaggerated, 39
flower images and number of
petals, 17–19
money, business, and career
factors, 38–39
as one of seven main
chakras, 16

position of, 37
problems related to, 93
topics associated with, 37–38
Soul, chakras and, 23
Spinal chakras, 62, 64
Spirituality, 85. *See also* Energy
and spiritual healing

Tenth chakra, 109
Theosophical Society, 13
Therapies, overview of, 8–9
Third eye. *See* Brow chakra
("third eye")
Throat chakra, **47–51**
about: overview of functions
and associations, 17–23
of animals, 134
balanced, 48
body and health associations,
50
checklist for identifying
weaknesses, 69
color of and healing with
color, 20, 108
correspondences/
connections, 51, 137
crystals for clearing, 103
deficient or damaged, 50
details and key ideas, 47
elements and, 71
emotional pain/problems
and healing methods,
120–121
essential oils for, 114, 115, 135
exaggerated, 49
flower images and number of
petals, 17–19
money, business, and career
factors, 48–49
as one of seven main
chakras, 16
position of, 47
problems related to, 93
topics associated with, 47–48
Tiger's eye, 101
Turquoise blue, healing with,
108, 124
Twelfth chakra, 109

Upanishads, chakras and, 13

Vedic names of chakras, 136–137
Vegetables, color of, chakras
and, 106

Warnings, 23
Water element/signs, 71, 128
White, healing with, 109, 124,
126

Yellow, healing with, 108, 124,
126

Zodiac sign connections,
136–137